THE LITTLE GUIDES

LOW-CARB

THE LITTLE GUIDES

LOW-CARB

FOG CITY PRESS

Published by Fog City Press
814 Montgomery Street
San Francisco, CA 94133 USA
Reprinted in 2004 (twice)

Copyright © 2004 Weldon Owen Pty Ltd

Chief Executive Officer: John Owen
President: Terry Newell
Publisher: Lynn Humphries
Managing Editor: Janine Flew
Design Manager: Helen Perks
Editorial Coordinator: Jennifer Losco
Production Manager: Caroline Webber
Production Coordinator: James Blackman
Sales Manager: Emily Jahn
Vice President International Sales: Stuart Laurence

Project Editor: Ariana Klepac
Project Designer: Jacqueline Richards

A catalog record for this book is available from
the Library of Congress, Washington, DC.

ISBN 1 877019 92 5

Color reproduction by Colourscan Co Pte Ltd
Printed by SNP LeeFung Printers Limited (China)
Printed in China

A Weldon Owen Production

HEALTH ADVISORY
This is a cookbook, not a diet book. The
information it contains is general, not specific to
individuals and their particular circumstances. If you
or a member of your family has a pre-existing health
condition, is on medication, or has specific dietary
requirements, you should consult a qualified medical
practitioner before significantly changing your diet.
The publishers cannot be held responsible for
any illness or adverse reaction resulting from
adherence to a low-carbohydrate diet.

CONTENTS

■ **LOW-CARBOHYDRATE EATING**   8

■ **PROTEIN**   10

■ **FATS**   12

■ **CARBOHYDRATES**   14

■ **CALCIUM**   16

■ **TASTE**   17

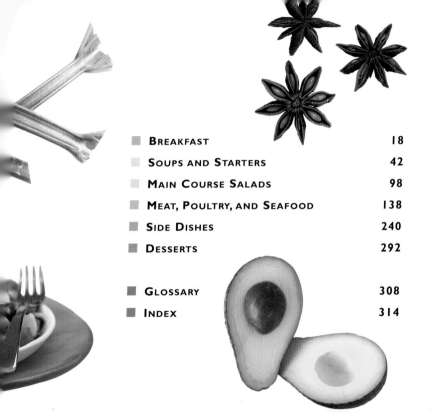

▪ **BREAKFAST**		18
▪ **SOUPS AND STARTERS**		42
▪ **MAIN COURSE SALADS**		98
▪ **MEAT, POULTRY, AND SEAFOOD**		138
▪ **SIDE DISHES**		240
▪ **DESSERTS**		292
▪ **GLOSSARY**		308
▪ **INDEX**		314

Low-Carbohydrate Eating

Everything that we can safely eat or drink contains energy, or fuel, to keep our bodies working. This fuel is measured as calories or kilojoules.

Logically, it is the balance of fuel *in* (total calories eaten), and fuel *out* (the total fuel used up keeping the body functioning in the equivalent time) that determines whether we store fuel (put on weight) or need extra fuel (and therefore shed weight).

There is some good news for the health conscious, since we now know that not all calories have the same effect. It appears that excess calories obtained from carbohydrates (for example, bread, pasta, and rice) are more readily converted into fat stores than those from other foods, such as protein (meat, poultry, and seafood). Often the body's daily need for carbohydrate is exceeded. Fortunately, protein foods tend to be more satisfying and sustaining than carbohydrates, and also enable more effective usage of fat stores.

It is these food facts that are the fundamentals for the more recent approaches to dieting, where total carbohydrate is restricted and protein foods are favored.

No matter what type of food is favored, from the point of view of satisfaction and using up fat stores, there is still a minimum "nutrient" requirement to be met from daily food intake, which cannot be ignored. Put simply, it is no good being slim but otherwise unhealthy. Therefore it is important to look both at the quantities of any foods eaten, as well as the different food types required. This will achieve weight control as well as enhance general good health.

Haloumi and Vegetable Kabobs
(see page 83)

9

Protein

We need protein from our food daily to provide the "building blocks" to enable our bodies to repair themselves. The advantage of protein-rich foods from animal sources (meats, poultry, and seafood) is that not only are they excellent sources of a wide range of nutrients essential for health and vitality, they can also be very lean and, as stated previously, they are the most satisfying.

Stuffed Chicken Breasts with Bell Pepper Coulis (see page 184)

This is the big bonus—protein-rich foods keep hunger at bay for much longer than many other foods. Therefore, it is much easier to stick to a high-protein eating plan for longer than to one which is mainly carbohydrate-based and leaves you desperate to raid the cookie jar between meals.

The leaner types of proteins are the best to select from. See the box opposite for details.

INCLUDE	INCLUDE SOMETIMES	AVOID
Lean beef, veal, lamb, pork	Cheese	Regular sausages
Lean ham	Pulses, such as kidney beans, cannellini beans, chick peas, lentils	Salami
Skinless chicken, turkey		Pressed chicken
Lean game	Trimmed bacon	Pressed ham
All seafood	Low-fat sausages	Spam
Eggs	Fried tofu	
Tofu		
Ricotta cheese		

Fats

Excess fats, whether they come from added fats used in cooking or manufacturing, or from the fats that are an integral part of food, are easily converted to body fat. This is because they

require little or no further processing to be placed in the body's fat stores. It may seem logical to think that by eliminating all fats you will avoid putting on weight, but unfortunately this is not the case. No-fat diets are totally inadequate. There are certain essential fats that the body cannot manufacture itself, so no-fat diets are not nutritionally balanced. Indeed, for a dieter they are disastrous, since the fat shortage signals to the body to firmly hold onto whatever body fat it already has. To function properly, the body *needs* some fat, particularly those fats that it cannot manufacture itself.

Therefore, both the quantity and type of fats used are important.

Previous low-carbohydrate diets suggested a liberal use of all types of fats. This has proven not to be healthy, since excess fats cause rocketing cholesterol levels, exacerbate blood pressure problems, and may even be linked to an increased risk of certain cancers.

The ideal scenario, therefore, is to avoid excessive fat intake, to use the preferred fat sources to add flavor and taste to foods (see the box opposite), and to ensure that all protein foods used are 100 percent lean.

INCLUDE	INCLUDE SOMETIMES	AVOID
Canola oil	Cheese	Processed foods
Olive oil	Cream	Butter, margarine, ghee
Avocado	Sour cream	Vegetable oils, such as sunflower and safflower oil
Nuts and seeds: almonds, cashews, hazelnuts (filberts), walnuts, sesame seeds, pine nuts	Peanuts	Cookies and cakes
	Peanut oil	Fried foods
	Pecans	

Carbohydrates

Carbohydrates are an essential fuel for the body. However, too much carbohydrate can quickly overload the system, which immediately causes the body to turn the excess carbohydrate into stored fat.

Think of carbohydrates as fat "lighter fuel." The body requires small amounts of carbohydrate to start up the metabolism, which then enables fat stores to be used effectively.

As with fats, there are some carbohydrates which are more appropriate than others, being better fat firelighters. Therefore, eating small amounts of the better types of carbohydrates should encourage the use of stored fat in the body.

In addition, carbohydrates contain important vitamins and minerals that are not present in such concentrated amounts in other foods. Therefore, the best fat-burning diet is a *low* carbo-

hydrate diet, rather than a *no-*carbohydrate diet.

Sugar often plays an important taste role in certain foods. Therefore, in this book, small amounts of sugar have been included as an optional ingredient in some recipes. An alternative is to replace some or all of the sugar in a recipe with one of the many artificial sweeteners available, to the required equivalent sweetness of sugar.

INCLUDE	INCLUDE SOMETIMES	AVOID
	Grain crispbreads Grain breads	All other bread-type products Pastries, cakes, and cookies Processed foods containing sugar
	Coarse country (wholegrain) bread Thickeners	Cereals, couscous, flours, noodles, pasta, and rice Potatoes
All vegetables and salad items except those listed	Corn, peas, and sweet potatoes	
All fresh fruits in appropriate quantities; for health, 2 serves per day should be eaten	Preserved fruits in own juice	Preserved fruits in syrup
	Beans, pulses, and legumes	
2 quarts (2 l) water, mineral water, or soda water per day	Diet soft drinks	Drinks containing sugar

Calcium

Calcium is one nutrient that requires a special mention, because it is found in one of the first food groups to be reduced in a low-carbohydrate diet—the dairy foods or dairy substitute group.

This is a significant problem because, when protein intakes are high, the body has a greater difficulty retaining calcium. (This can be measured by the amount of calcium found in the urine.)

Since retaining calcium in the body and bone structure is vital for long-term bone strength, it is important that there is a daily intake of high-calcium dairy foods, or fortified high-calcium dairy substitutes.

Hard cheese is a useful source of calcium, because it contains no carbohydrates (the milk carbohydrate, lactose, being

discarded when the whey is separated off during production). But, unfortunately, cheese is particularly high in the less-preferable saturated fats, so it is not to be consumed in unlimited amounts. The low-fat hard cheeses tend to have carbohydrate added to replace the fats.

The aim therefore, is to include, on a daily basis, a minimum of 1¾ oz (50 g) of cheese and 1¼ cups (10 fl oz/300 ml) of high-calcium, low-fat dairy or dairy substitute, or ¾ cup (6½ fl oz/200 ml) of yogurt.

Taste

Eating on a low-carbohydrate diet does not have to be boring. Remember that one tasty, high-protein meal is more likely to satisfy you, than continually snacking on boring, tasteless foods. Therefore, it is important to make use of the wide range of herbs, spices, and sauces available to enhance your food.

Be adventurous with herbs and spices in your cooking. A simple dish can be made more flavorful and tempting with the use of just a few chopped fresh herbs added at the end of cooking time.

Chicken Wings with Barbecue Sauce
(see page 44)

The recipes in this book cover a wide range of cooking styles, techniques, and international cuisines. From tasty starters such as Spicy Spanish Kabobs, to satisfying main courses such as Italian Chicken with Pesto

Mayonnaise, to delectable desserts such as Raspberry Parfait, you will find plenty of tasty ideas to help make your everyday low-carbohydrate eating an enjoyable as well as a healthy experience.

17

BREAKFAST

Classic Omelets with Fines Herbes and Tomato Concasse

TOMATO CONCASSE

3 tablespoons extra virgin olive oil

3 tablespoons finely diced shallots

2 tomatoes, seeded and finely diced, with juices

1 teaspoon salt

Ground black pepper

OMELETS

12 eggs

1 teaspoon salt

Ground black pepper

2 tablespoons extra virgin olive oil

2 tablespoons cold unsalted butter, cut into small pieces

4 teaspoons fresh fines herbes

Fresh chervil and thyme sprigs

To make the concasse, in a small nonreactive saucepan over medium heat, warm the olive oil. Add the shallots and sauté until wilted, about 45 seconds. Add the tomatoes and juices, the salt, and a pinch or two of pepper. Reduce the heat slightly and cook, stirring gently from time to time, until the tomato juices have evaporated, about 8–10 minutes. Remove from the heat and cover to keep warm.

To make the omelets, in a small bowl, beat the eggs until well blended. Season with salt and pepper to taste.

Place a 7- or 8-inch (18- or 20-cm) nonstick frying pan over medium heat. When the pan is hot, add $1/2$ tablespoon of the oil, heat briefly and pour in one-fourth of the beaten eggs. Sprinkle $1/2$ tablespoon of the butter pieces and 1 teaspoon of the fines herbes over the surface. Allow the eggs to cook, without stirring, for just 10 seconds then, using a wooden spoon, begin to pull the eggs away from the edges of the pan toward the center so that some of the uncooked egg runs underneath. Cook until the eggs are still somewhat moist on the surface,

but set and lightly browned on the bottom, 40–60 seconds. Using a small spatula, fold the omelet in half and gently slide it out of the pan onto a warmed individual plate. Repeat the process, wiping out the pan with paper towels before cooking the remaining 3 omelets.

Spoon some of the warm tomato concasse over each omelet and garnish with chervil and thyme sprigs. Serve immediately.

Serves 4

Breakfast BLT

4 slices (rashers) bacon

Vegetable oil, for greasing pan

2 eggs

4 flat lettuce leaves

1 tomato, cut into 4 slices

Preheat a broiler (griller).

Broil (grill) the bacon. Meanwhile, in a lightly greased frying pan, cook the eggs in egg rings.

Assemble the BLT on 2 separate plates. Layer in the following order: a lettuce leaf, a slice of bacon, an egg, 2 slices of tomato, a slice of bacon, and a lettuce leaf. Serve immediately.

Serves 2

Eggs Florentine

1 package (8 oz/250 g) frozen chopped spinach

1 1/2 tablespoons butter

1 1/2 tablespoons all-purpose (plain) flour

1 cup (8 fl oz/250 ml) milk

Salt

Ground black pepper

Grated nutmeg

1/4 cup (1 oz/30 g) grated Parmesan cheese

4 large eggs

Place the spinach in a small saucepan and cover tightly. Cook over low heat for about 8 minutes, removing the lid for the final 3 minutes to evaporate the liquid. Drain.

In another pan melt the butter, stir in the flour, then add the milk and whisk constantly to make a béchamel (white) sauce. Stir continually as it thickens. Season to taste with salt, pepper, and nutmeg, then stir in the well-drained spinach and the cheese. Set aside and keep warm.

Poach the eggs until the whites are set and the yolks still soft.

To serve, spoon a mound of creamed spinach onto each of 4 serving plates and make a well in the center. Remove the eggs with a slotted spoon and place 1 egg on each bed of spinach. Serve immediately.

NOTE: The béchamel sauce can be made up to 1 day in advance and kept in the refrigerator. Place a piece of plastic wrap or waxed paper directly on the surface of the sauce to prevent a skin from forming.

Serves 4

Curried Eggs

1 clove garlic, minced

1 tablespoon canola oil

1/2–1 teaspoon curry powder

4 eggs, beaten

2 tablespoons parsley, minced (to counteract the garlic)

Sauté the garlic in the oil until soft. Add the curry powder and cook, stirring, for 1 minute.

Add the eggs and stir over low heat until just set, then stir in the parsley. Serve immediately.

Serves 2

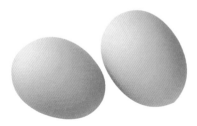

Smoked Salmon Stack

6 spinach leaves, wilted

4 slices smoked salmon

¼ cup (2 oz/60 g) cottage cheese

Fresh lemon juice

Ground black pepper

Assemble the salmon stacks on 2 separate plates. Layer in the following order: a spinach leaf, a slice of salmon, a tablespoon of cottage cheese, a spinach leaf, a slice of salmon, a tablespoon of cottage cheese, and the last spinach leaf. Top with a squeeze of lemon juice and black pepper to taste. Serve immediately.

Serves 2

Eggs Scrambled with Beans and Salsa

1 fresh poblano chili pepper

3 corn tortillas, each 6 inches (15 cm) in diameter

6 tablespoons (3 fl oz/100 ml) corn oil

1 cup (8 oz/250 g) refried beans

1/2 cup (2 oz/60 g) chopped white onion

1 fresh jalapeño chili pepper, seeded and finely diced

2 teaspoons chopped cilantro (fresh coriander), plus extra sprigs for garnish

8 eggs, beaten

3/4 teaspoon salt

1 cup (4 oz/125 g) shredded Monterey Jack cheese

1 cup (8 fl oz/250 ml) salsa

Preheat a broiler (griller). Place the poblano chili on the pan and place under the broiler. Broil (grill), turning as necessary, until charred on all sides. Remove from the broiler and let cool for 5 minutes, then remove the charred skin by peeling it away while holding the chili under cold, running water. Cut into small strips.

Stack the corn tortillas and cut them in half. Cut the halves into narrow triangular wedges. In a nonstick frying pan over medium heat, warm the corn oil. Add the tortilla pieces and sauté until slightly crisp, about 30 seconds. Using tongs or a slotted spoon, transfer to paper towels to drain. Reserve the pan and oil.

In a small saucepan over medium heat, reheat the refried beans; set aside and keep warm.

In the frying pan used for the corn tortillas, over medium heat, sauté the onion in the remaining oil until just tender, 3 minutes.

Add the corn tortilla strips, poblano, jalapeño, and chopped cilantro. Sauté briefly, then add the beaten eggs and the salt and stir with a wooden spoon for 10 seconds. Add 1/2 cup (2 oz/60 g) of the cheese and continue to stir until the eggs are just set yet still tender and moist, 15–20 seconds.

Divide the eggs evenly among 4 warmed individual plates. Place a spoonful of the refried beans alongside the eggs and

sprinkle with the remaining 1/2 cup (2 oz/60 g) cheese. Garnish with the cilantro sprigs and serve with the salsa.

Serves 4

Cheese and Egg Scramble with Chives and Bacon

3 slices (rashers) bacon, very finely shredded

6 eggs

2 tablespoons finely chopped chives

½ teaspoon salt

¼ teaspoon coarsely ground black pepper

¼ cup (1 oz/30 g) grated Cheddar cheese

2 slices wholewheat (wholemeal) or coarse country (wholegrain) bread, toasted and buttered

1 tomato, cut into 8 slices

Heat a small pan and sauté the bacon until it is lightly crisped. Remove the bacon from the pan with a slotted spoon.

Beat the eggs, adding half the chives, the salt and pepper, and the bacon, reserving a little for garnish. Stir in the cheese.

Pour the bacon drippings into an omelet pan or nonstick pan and heat to medium-hot. Pour in the egg mixture and stir slowly until it is just set.

Serve over ½ slice of buttered toast and garnish each serve with some of the remaining chives and bacon and 2 tomato slices.

Serves 4

Watermelon Frappé

1 cup (4 oz/125 g) seeded watermelon flesh, cubed

1½ oz (45 g) raspberries

1½ oz (45 g) strawberries

Sweetener, to taste

8 fl oz (250 ml) carbonated mineral water

½ cup (4 fl oz/125 ml) low-calorie (diet) lemon-lime soda

Place the watermelon, berries, and sweetener in a blender or the bowl of food processor and process until puréed. Transfer the purée to a freezer-proof bowl and add the mineral water and the lemon-lime soda. Place the frappé in the freezer and freeze until semi-set or fully frozen.

Remove the frappé from the freezer, and process in a blender or food processor until mushy. Pour into 2 serving glasses and serve immediately.

Serves 2

Sautéed Mushrooms and Bacon

1 package (¾ oz/20 g) dried porcini mushrooms

1 cup (8 fl oz/250 ml) cool water

1 tablespoon extra virgin olive oil

2 tablespoons minced yellow onion

1 tablespoon minced garlic

1 lb (500 g) assorted fresh mushrooms, stems removed, brushed clean, and sliced

¼ cup (½ oz/15 g) minced fresh parsley

¼ cup (2 fl oz/60 ml) dry Italian white wine

4 slices (rashers) bacon

Salt and ground black pepper

In a bowl, combine the porcini mushrooms and water. Let stand until softened, about 20 minutes. Remove the mushrooms, reserving the liquid. Clean the mushrooms, if needed, and chop coarsely. Strain the liquid through a fine-mesh sieve lined with cheesecloth (muslin) into a container, then discard all but ¼ cup (2 fl oz/ 60 ml) of the liquid.

In a frying pan over medium heat, warm the olive oil. When hot, add the onion and garlic and sauté for about 30 seconds; do not allow to brown. Add the porcini mushrooms and fresh mushrooms and continue to sauté, stirring continuously

to prevent burning, until slightly limp, about 3 minutes.

Add the ¼ cup (2 fl oz/60 ml) reserved porcini liquid and simmer for 3 minutes. Add the parsley and white wine and simmer over medium heat until there is only ¼ cup (2 fl oz/ 60 ml) liquid remaining, about 8–10 minutes.

Meanwhile, cook the bacon until done to your liking.

Season the mushrooms to taste with salt and pepper. Transfer them to warmed serving plates and serve with the bacon.

Serves 4

The Importance of Fiber

M any of the carbohydrate foods that we avoid in a low-carbohydrate diet are often the major sources of fiber in a regular diet. Therefore, a change to low-carbohydrate eating can be a major challenge to the body, which is used to functioning on larger amounts of fiber.

Different types of fiber are necessary in the diet for various reasons. Certain fibers provide "food" for the various micro-organisms in the lower gut. Inadequate amounts of these fibers cause the micro-organisms to decrease in number, which can result in decreased gut activity, lower resistance to infection, and loss of protection against certain cancers. Other fibers are not digested at all, and pass through the lower gut intact, contributing significantly to the final bulk of the body's waste products. The greater the bulk passing through the gut system, the easier it is for the system to work efficiently. Therefore, low fiber intake causes long-term gut stress.

Fiber is found in vegetables and salad items, as well as fruits, grain products, and legumes. The fruit, vegetable, and salad fibers are different from those found in grains and legumes. Therefore, although it is recommended to include 2 servings of fruit, and at least 2–3 cups of the lower-carbohydrate vegetables and salad items per day, this still may not meet all the body's daily fiber needs. Therefore it may be necessary to include dishes with added cereal bran.

Grain bran contains fiber, but very small amounts of carbohydrate, so it is perfect for a low-carbohydrate eating plan. Oat bran and wheat bran are particularly effective, as are psyllium husks.

Easy Crab Patties

1 cup (8 oz/250 g) canned or thawed, frozen crabmeat

1 clove garlic, minced

1 tablespoon minced parsley

1/2 tablespoon minced dill

1 egg

1 tablespoon oat bran

1/3 cup (1 1/2 oz/45 g) grated Parmesan cheese

Ground black pepper to taste

Olive oil

Combine all the ingredients, except the oil, in a bowl and mix until well blended. Form the mixture into small, flattened balls.

In a nonstick frying pan heat a little oil and lightly fry the patties until golden brown. Serve immediately.

Serves 1 to 2

Strawberry Cream Smoothie

½ cup (4 fl oz/125 ml) light (single) cream

2 tablespoons cottage cheese

⅓ cup (2½ oz/80 g) crushed ice

½ cup (2 oz/60 g) strawberries

½ tablespoon oat or wheat bran

Mint leaves, to decorate

In a blender, purée the cream, cottage cheese, and ice. Add the strawberries and blend again, until the strawberries are partially blended.

Serve the smoothie in a tall glass with mint leaves to decorate.

Serves 1 to 2

Eggs Benedict with Virginia Ham

HOLLANDAISE SAUCE

4 egg yolks

2 teaspoons fresh lemon juice

1 teaspoon chopped shallot

1 teaspoon white wine vinegar

1 1/4 teaspoons salt

1 1/2 tablespoons water

Pinch of cayenne pepper

1 cup (8 oz/250 g) butter, melted

2 teaspoons salt

2 tablespoons distilled white vinegar

8 eggs

6 oz (190 g) Virginia ham, thinly sliced

Fresh chives

To make the hollandaise sauce, in a stainless-steel bowl, combine the egg yolks, lemon juice, shallot, vinegar, and salt. Place over (but not touching) simmering water in a pan. Whisk continuously until the mixture is pale lemon yellow and falls in thick ribbons when the whisk is lifted, about 5 minutes. Remove the sauce from the heat and whisk in the water and cayenne pepper. Then, whisking continuously, slowly drizzle in the butter until all of it has been used and a thick emulsion has formed. Cover the sauce and keep warm.

Pour water into a large frying pan to a depth of 3 inches (7.5 cm) and bring to a boil. Adjust the heat so the water is just below boiling point. Add the salt and vinegar. One at a time, crack the eggs into a small ramekin or tea cup and gently lower into the water. Work as quickly as possible, so that all the eggs will cook in about the same amount of time. Cook until the whites are firm but the yolks are still soft, 3–4 minutes. Using a slotted spoon, transfer the eggs to a paper towel-lined platter to drain. Trim away any straggly strands of egg.

On each warmed individual plate, place an equal amount of the ham and a poached egg. Spoon the hollandaise sauce over the top, garnish with the chives, and serve immediately.

Serves 4

Ricotta Cheese Scramble

¼ cup (2 fl oz/60 ml) safflower oil

1 onion, minced

4–5 fresh serrano chilies, or to taste, minced

8 oz (250 g) tomatoes, unpeeled and finely chopped

2½ cups (1¼ lb/600 g) ricotta cheese

½ teaspoon sea salt, or to taste

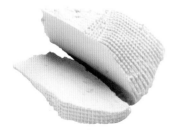

Heat the oil in a frying pan and add the onion and chilies. Fry gently without browning for 1 minute. Add the tomatoes and cook over high heat, stirring occasionally, for 4 minutes, or until the mixture is fairly dry. Add the ricotta and salt, and mix well. Cook over medium heat for about 4 minutes, or until the mixture begins to turn a light golden color and comes away cleanly from the surface of the pan when turned with a spoon.

Place on 4 warmed serving plates and serve immediately.

Serves 4

SOUPS AND STARTERS

Chicken Wings with Barbecue Sauce

6 cups (1½ qt/1.5 l) olive oil, for deep-frying

18 small chicken wings (about 2½ lb/1.25 kg total)

3 tablespoons (1½ oz/45 g) butter

⅔ cup (5 fl oz/160 ml) hot barbecue sauce

½ cup (4 fl oz/125 ml) light sour cream

3 oz (100 g) blue cheese, crumbled

Coarsely cracked black pepper to taste

1 green (spring) onion, finely chopped

Dash of lemon juice

3 large stalks celery, cut into 2-inch (5-cm) sticks (optional)

In a large saucepan, heat the oil to 365°F (185°C). Deep-fry the chicken wings until golden and crisp, about 15 minutes. Remove and drain.

In a small pan over medium heat, melt the butter. Add the barbecue sauce and stir until smooth. Keep hot.

Combine the sour cream, blue cheese, pepper, green onion, and lemon juice and mix to make a smooth dip. Spoon into a small serving dish.

Pour the barbecue sauce over the chicken, brushing each piece so it is thickly and evenly coated. Place the dip in the center of a wide serving dish and surround with the chicken. If desired, decorate dish with the celery, or serve separately.

Serves 6

Spicy Spanish Kabobs

1/4 cup (2 fl oz/60 ml) olive oil

1 tablespoon lemon juice

2 tablespoons chopped flat-leaf (Italian) parsley, plus extra sprigs for garnish

1/2 teaspoon ground cumin

1/4–1/2 teaspoon cayenne pepper

1/2 teaspoon dried thyme, crushed

1/2 teaspoon paprika

1/8 teaspoon saffron threads, crushed, or ground turmeric

Salt and ground black pepper

12 oz (375 g) chicken thigh meat, cut into 1-inch (2.5-cm) cubes or 2- × 1-inch (5- × 2.5-cm) strips

1 large orange, cut into segments, for garnish

Combine the oil, lemon juice, parsley, cumin, cayenne pepper, thyme, paprika, saffron or turmeric, and salt and pepper. Pour the mixture into a strong plastic bag, add the chicken, seal bag, and turn to coat the chicken evenly. Refrigerate for 4–24 hours, turning the bag from time to time. Drain, reserving marinade.

Turn on broiler (griller). Thread chicken pieces on 4 long metal skewers, leaving about 1/4 inch (5 mm) between each one. Place the kabobs on the unheated rack of the broiler pan. Broil (grill) 3–4 inches (7.5–10 cm) from heat until chicken is cooked through, 10–12 minutes, turning once and brushing with reserved marinade occasionally during cooking. Garnish with parsley sprigs and orange segments.

Serves 4

Fish Cakes with Pickled Cucumber Relish

PICKLED CUCUMBER
RELISH

1/3 cup (2 1/2 fl oz/80 ml) distilled
white vinegar

1 teaspoon salt

1/4 cup (2 fl oz/60 ml) water

Sweetener, equivalent to
2 tablespoons sugar

1 English (hothouse) cucumber

1 large shallot, thinly sliced

1 fresh small red chili, seeded
and chopped

1 teaspoon dried shrimp (prawn)
powder (optional)

1 tablespoon coarsely chopped
cilantro (fresh coriander)

1 tablespoon coarsely chopped
dry-roasted peanuts

FISH CAKES

1 lb (500 g) salmon fillets or
whitefish paste

1 tablespoon Thai fish sauce

2 teaspoons Thai roasted
chili paste (nam prik pao) or
1 1/2 teaspoons red curry paste

1 egg, lightly beaten

1/4 teaspoon salt

1/2 tablespoon cornstarch
(cornflour)

4 oz (125 g) green beans,
trimmed and cut crosswise into
slices 1/8 inch (3 mm) thick

2 tablespoons coarsely chopped
cilantro (fresh coriander)

Peanut or vegetable oil, for frying

To make the cucumber relish, in a saucepan over medium heat, combine the vinegar, salt, and water. Bring to a simmer, stirring to dissolve the salt. Remove from the heat and let cool. Add the sweetener.

Peel the cucumber and cut in half lengthwise. Cut it crosswise into very thin slices and place it in a bowl. Add the shallot, chili, dried shrimp powder (if using), and cilantro and stir to mix well. Pour the vinegar dressing over the cucumber mixture and set aside. Just before serving, sprinkle the peanuts on top.

To make the fish cakes, if using fillets, cut the fish into 1-inch (2.5-cm) cubes and place in a food processor fitted with the metal blade. Process until a fairly smooth paste forms. Transfer to a large bowl. If using whitefish paste, simply place in the bowl. Add the fish sauce, chili or curry paste, egg, salt, cornstarch, green beans, and cilantro. Stir to mix well.

Moisten your hands with water and form the mixture into about 24 cakes each about 2 inches (5 cm) in diameter and 1/2 inch (1 cm) thick. As the cakes are formed, set them on an oiled baking sheet.

In a frying pan over medium-high heat, pour in oil to a depth of 1 inch (2.5 cm) and heat to 375°F (190°C) on a deep-frying thermometer. Using an oiled slotted spatula, lower a few fish cakes into the oil and fry, turning once, until golden brown and crisp, about 2 minutes per side. Transfer to paper towels to drain. Place on a platter and keep warm while frying the remaining fish cakes.

To serve, divide the cucumber relish among individual dipping saucers. Arrange 3 or 4 cakes on each serving plate and place a saucer of the cucumber relish alongside. Serve warm.

Makes about 24 fish cakes; serves 8 to 12

Fresh Tomato and Thyme Soup

1 tablespoon olive oil

2 cloves garlic, minced, plus 3 whole cloves

2 onions, chopped

4 lb (2 kg) tomatoes, peeled and chopped

1 tablespoon tomato paste

1 teaspoon sugar (optional)

1 bay leaf

4 large sprigs fresh thyme, plus 6 small sprigs for garnish (optional)

1/2 teaspoon Tabasco sauce

Salt and ground pepper

1/2 cup (4 fl oz/125 ml) vegetable or chicken stock

Heat the oil in a saucepan over medium heat. Add the minced garlic and the onions and cook, stirring, for 5 minutes, or until the onions are soft. Stir in the tomatoes, tomato paste, sugar (if using), bay leaf, large thyme sprigs, whole garlic cloves, Tabasco sauce, salt and pepper to taste, and stock. Simmer, uncovered, for 20 minutes or until the tomatoes are soft and the liquid has reduced by about one third.

Remove and discard the bay leaf, thyme, and garlic cloves. Blend or process the soup until smooth, then return it to the pan and reheat. Serve the soup garnished with the small sprigs of thyme, if desired.

Serves 6

51

Sour Fish Soup

1 whole catfish, striped bass, sea bass, or red snapper (about 2 lb/1 kg)

1 tablespoon fish sauce

1/4 teaspoon ground black pepper

1 green (spring) onion, thinly sliced

FISH SOUP

1 tablespoon vegetable oil

2 shallots, thinly sliced

3 lemongrass stalks, cut into 2-inch (5-cm) lengths and crushed

6 cups (48 fl oz/1.5 l) water or chicken stock

2 oz (60 g) tamarind pulp, chopped

1 cup (8 fl oz/250 ml) boiling water

1 cup (6 oz/190 g) diced pineapple

1/3 cup (1 1/2 oz/45 g) drained, sliced, canned bamboo shoots

2 small fresh red chilis, seeded and thinly sliced

1 teaspoon sugar (optional)

2 tablespoons fish sauce, or to taste

2 small, firm tomatoes, cut into wedges

1 cup (2 oz/60 g) bean sprouts

Salt and ground black pepper

Cilantro (fresh coriander) sprigs or sliced fresh mint leaves, for garnishing

1 lime, cut into wedges

If the fish is not already cleaned, use a sharp knife to slit the fish open from the vent (the tiny hole in the belly) to the head. Empty the cavity of all the guts and scrape away any dark blood from the backbone. Rinse the cavity well. Using the back of a heavy knife, scrape the scales away from the fish, working from the tail toward the head. Rinse and dry the fish well.

Remove the fish head and use a thin, flexible knife to carefully cut between the fillet and the backbone, working from the tail up. Remove the fish fillet, then turn the fish over and repeat to remove the remaining fillet. Reserve the fish head, bones, and any scraps. Cut the fillets into 1-inch (2.5-cm) cubes and place in a bowl with the fish sauce, pepper, and green onion. Toss gently to combine, then set the mixture aside at room temperature to marinate.

For the fish soup, heat the vegetable oil in a large saucepan over medium heat. When the oil is hot, add the fish head, bones, and scraps and stir to combine. Add the shallots and lemongrass and cook gently, stirring often,

until fragrant, 3–5 minutes. Do not let the mixture brown. Add the water or chicken stock and bring to a boil. Reduce the heat to low and simmer, uncovered, for 20 minutes.

Meanwhile, in a small bowl soak the tamarind pulp in the boiling water for 15 minutes. Mash the tamarind pulp using the back of a fork to help it dissolve. Carefully pour the mixture through a fine-mesh sieve into another small bowl, pressing against the tamarind pulp to extract as much of the flavorful liquid as possible. Discard the pulp and set the liquid aside.

Pour the stock through a fine-mesh sieve into a large saucepan. Discard the contents of the sieve.

Bring the stock to a boil. Stir in the tamarind liquid, pineapple, bamboo shoots, chilis, sugar (if using), and fish sauce. Reduce the heat to medium and simmer for 1 minute. Add the tomatoes and marinated fish and continue to simmer until the fish is opaque and feels firm to the touch, 3–5 minutes. Add the bean sprouts and season with salt and pepper to taste.

Serve immediately, garnished with cilantro or mint, and accompanied by the lime wedges.

Serves 4 to 6

Sicilian Vegetable Soup

2 lb (1 kg) medium eggplants (aubergines)

1/3 cup (2½ fl oz/80 ml) olive oil

1 lb (500 g) onions, thinly sliced

1 lb (500 g) ripe tomatoes, seeded and cut into strips

2 tablespoons capers, rinsed

2–3 stalks celery, chopped

6 oz (190 g) black olives, pitted

2 cups (16 fl oz/500 ml) tomato juice

2 cups (16 fl oz/500 ml) vegetable or chicken stock

1/3 cup (2½ fl oz/80 ml) vinegar (use any kind)

1 teaspoon sugar (optional)

Wash the eggplants and cut them into small pieces. Set aside.

Meanwhile, heat a third of the olive oil in a large frying pan. Add the onions and cook, stirring, until golden. Stir in the tomatoes, capers, celery, and olives and cook for 15 minutes. Set aside.

Rinse the eggplant pieces and dry thoroughly on paper towels. Heat the remaining oil in a frying pan over high heat. When the oil reaches its maximum temperature, add the eggplant and fry until well browned. Drain on paper towels.

Stir the fried eggplant into the tomato mixture. Add the tomato juice, stock, vinegar, and sugar (if using). Return to low heat and cook until the ingredients are heated through. Serve hot.

Serves 4

Fish Soup

2 lb (1 kg) mussels in the shells

4 lb (2 kg) assorted firm fish fillets (such as bass, flounder, halibut, haddock, snapper, cod, and grouper)

1/2 cup (4 fl oz/125 ml) olive oil

2 cups (7 oz/220 g) sliced yellow onions

1 cup (3 oz/100 g) sliced leeks, washed well

4 cloves garlic, minced

2 celery stalks, chopped

1 1/2 cups (9 oz/275 g) peeled, seeded, and chopped tomatoes (fresh or canned)

4 sprigs fresh thyme

1 bay leaf

1/2 cup (3/4 oz/20 g) chopped fresh flat-leaf (Italian) parsley

1 cup (8 fl oz/250 ml) dry white wine

7 cups (56 fl oz/1.75 l) water

1 lb (500 g) uncooked shrimp (prawns), peeled and deveined

Fresh lemon juice

Salt and ground black pepper

Discard any mussels that do not close when lightly touched. Scrub the mussels under cold running water and remove their beards. Place in a bowl and refrigerate until needed.

Cut the fish fillets into 2-inch (5-cm) pieces. Place on a plate and refrigerate until needed.

Heat the olive oil in a large saucepan over medium heat. Add the onions and leeks and cook, stirring often, until they are translucent, about 8 minutes. Stir in the garlic, celery, tomato, thyme, bay leaf, and half of the parsley. Cook, stirring often, for 2 minutes.

Add the wine and water and bring the mixture to a boil over high heat. Reduce the heat to medium and simmer for 15 minutes. Stir in the salted fish pieces, cover, and cook for 5 minutes. Stir in the shrimp and mussels, cover, and cook until the mussels open, about 3–4 minutes. Discard any mussels that have not opened.

Season with lemon juice, and salt and pepper to taste. Serve immediately, sprinkled with the remaining parsley.

Serves 6

Shrimp with Fresh Herbs

2 lb (1 kg) uncooked medium shrimp (prawns), peeled and deveined

1 clove garlic, crushed

1/4 cup (2 fl oz/60 ml) olive oil

Salt and ground black pepper

1 bunch fresh flat-leaf (Italian) parsley

1 1/2 oz (45 g) fresh marjoram

1 1/2 oz (45 g) fresh thyme

1 1/2 oz (45 g) fresh tarragon

1 1/2 oz (45 g) fresh basil

1/4 cup (2 fl oz/60 ml) dry white wine

Finely chop all of the parsley, and half of each of the other herbs.

Fry the garlic gently in the oil until golden brown, then remove it. Add the shrimp to the oil and cook, stirring, until they turn pink and curl up, 2–3 minutes. Season with salt and pepper, then stir in the chopped herbs and the wine. Cook, stirring, for 3–4 minutes longer, then divide among serving plates.

Serve hot, garnished with the remaining fresh herbs.

Serves 4

Spicy Lamb Soup

SPICE PASTE

1 piece fresh ginger, 1 inch (2.5 cm) long, peeled and coarsely chopped

6 cloves garlic

6 purple (Asian) shallots, about 8 oz (250 g), cut in halves

1 1/2 teaspoons ground fennel

1 1/2 teaspoons ground cumin

1 tablespoon ground coriander

3 tablespoons water, or as needed

SOUP

1 1/2 lb (750 g) meaty lamb bones, for stock

12 cups (3 qt/3 l) water or meat stock

2 tablespoons canola oil

2 leeks, including 1 inch (2.5 cm) of the tender green tops, washed and sliced

1 teaspoon curry powder

2 cardamom pods, bruised

2 star anise

1 cinnamon stick

4 cloves

1 large carrot, peeled and thickly sliced

1 teaspoon sugar (optional)

1 1/2 teaspoons salt

1 beefsteak (large) tomato, cut into large wedges

Fresh lime juice (optional))

For the spice paste, place the ginger, garlic, shallots, fennel, cumin, and coriander in a blender. Blend to a smooth paste, adding the water as needed to assist blending. Set aside.

For the soup, preheat an oven to 450°F (220°C/Gas Mark 6). Remove any meat from the lamb bones, cut into 1-inch (2.5-cm) cubes, and set aside. Place the bones in a roasting pan and roast, turning occasionally, until browned, about 20 minutes. Transfer the bones to a plate and set aside.

Drain off the fat from the roasting pan and place the pan over medium heat. When the pan is hot, add 2 cups (16 fl oz/500 ml) of the water

or stock and deglaze the pan by stirring to dislodge any browned bits from the base. Set aside.

Heat the oil in a large stockpot over medium heat. Add the leeks and cook, stirring often, until golden, about 2 minutes. Add the spice paste and curry powder and stir until fragrant, about 1 minute. Add the roasted bones, reserved meat, the liquid from the roasting pan, and the remaining water or stock. Wrap the cardamom, star anise, cinnamon, and cloves in a piece of cheesecloth (muslin), tie securely with kitchen string, and add to the pan. Bring to a boil, then reduce the heat to low and simmer, uncovered, for 30 minutes. Stir in the carrot and simmer until the meat is

tender, about 30 minutes. Season with sugar (if using) and salt, and stir in the tomato.

Discard the cheesecloth bag and the bones and ladle the soup into serving bowls. Add lime juice to taste, if desired, and serve hot.

Serves 8

Clear Broth with Grilled Seafood

6 cups (48 fl oz/1.5 l) fish stock

8 oz (250 g) sea scallops

8 oz (250 g) uncooked shrimp (prawns), peeled and deveined

1–2 tablespoons olive oil

Salt and white pepper

Fresh chives, snipped into 1-inch (2.5-cm) lengths

Preheat a broiler (griller) or a gas or electric grill until very hot, or prepare a fire in a charcoal grill (barbecue).

In a saucepan, bring the fish stock to a boil over medium heat. Reduce the heat to very low and cover the pan.

Meanwhile, brush the scallops and shrimp with the olive oil and season lightly with salt and pepper. Place the seafood on an unheated broiler (griller) rack and broil close to the heat source until well seared and barely cooked through, 1–2 minutes per side.

When the seafood is almost done, ladle the hot stock into warmed large, shallow soup plates, taking care not to fill them all the way. Neatly place the pieces of seafood in the stock; they should protrude slightly above the surface of the liquid. Float the chives in the stock and serve immediately.

Serves 4 to 6

Tomato and Bell Pepper Soup with Chili Cream

2 red bell peppers (capsicums)

2 tablespoons oil

1 large onion, chopped

2 cloves garlic, chopped

3/4 cup (6 fl oz/190 ml) sherry

8 medium tomatoes, peeled and seeded

4 cups (32 fl oz/1 liter) chicken stock

1 bay leaf

3 sprigs fresh thyme

1 sprig fresh basil

1 large sprig fresh parsley

1 tablespoon black peppercorns

1 cup (8 fl oz/250 ml) heavy (double) cream

Juice of 1/2 lemon

Salt and ground black pepper

CHILI CREAM

1 long fresh green chili

1 clove garlic

5 spinach leaves, blanched in hot water

1/3 cup (2 1/2 fl oz/80 ml) heavy (double) cream, well chilled

1 tablespoon fresh lime juice

Salt and ground black pepper

Cook the bell peppers under a hot broiler (griller), turning occasionally, until the skin blisters and blackens. Place in a heatproof bowl, cover with plastic wrap, and set aside for approximately 10 minutes. Peel and roughly chop.

Heat the oil in a large saucepan. Add the onion and garlic and cook until softened. Add the sherry and cook until it evaporates. Stir in the tomatoes and stock. Tie the herbs and peppercorns in a square of cheesecloth (muslin) and add to the pan. Cook for 10 minutes, or until the mixture has reduced by a third. Stir in the cream and bell peppers. Simmer for 15 minutes, or until the liquid reduces slightly. Remove and discard the cheesecloth bag. Transfer to a food processor and process until smooth. Add the lemon juice and season to taste with salt and pepper.

For the chili cream, place the chili, garlic, and spinach in a food processor and process until smooth. Add the cream and process until combined. Add the lime juice and season with salt and pepper. Serve soup topped with a dollop of chili cream.

Serves 4 to 6

Asparagus with Dijon-Herb Mayonnaise

1 lb (500 g) asparagus

DIJON-HERB MAYONNAISE

1 large egg

4 teaspoons fresh lemon juice

1 tablespoon finely chopped fresh basil or 1 teaspoon dried basil, crushed

1 tablespoon finely chopped fresh thyme or 1 teaspoon dried thyme, crushed

1 tablespoon Dijon mustard

1/2 teaspoon salt

1 cup (8 fl oz/250 ml) extra virgin olive oil or salad oil

For the mayonnaise, in a blender or food processor, combine the egg, lemon juice, basil, thyme, mustard, and salt. Blend for 5 seconds. With the machine running at high speed, gradually add the oil in a fine stream through the feed tube or the hole in the lid, blending until smooth.

Prepare the asparagus by bending each spear; discard the woody bases where the spears snap easily.

Place the asparagus in the top of a double boiler or in a steamer basket over water in a saucepan. Cover and steam until crisp-tender, 5–6 minutes. Divide the spears among 4 serving plates; spoon over some of the mayonnaise.

Any leftover mayonnaise may be refrigerated in an airtight container for up to 1 week.

Serves 4

Seafood Gazpacho

4 tomatoes, peeled, seeded, and finely chopped

1 medium cucumber, peeled, seeded, and finely chopped

1 pimiento or small red bell pepper (capsicum), peeled, seeded, and finely chopped

1 small yellow bell pepper (capsicum), peeled, seeded, and finely chopped

1 red (Spanish) onion, finely chopped

2 cloves garlic, minced

Dash of hot-pepper sauce, such as Tabasco

1 teaspoon ground cumin

Juice of 1 lime

4 cups (32 fl oz/1 liter) tomato juice

2 tablespoons balsamic vinegar

1/2 cup (4 fl oz/125 ml) olive oil

Salt and pepper

1/4 cup (1/4 oz/7 g) chopped cilantro (fresh coriander)

1 avocado, peeled, pitted, and finely chopped

1 cup (8 oz/250 g) chopped combined shrimp (prawn) and crab meat

Cilantro (fresh coriander) leaves, to serve

Combine the tomato, cucumber, pimiento, bell pepper, and onion in a large bowl. Add the garlic, hot-pepper sauce, cumin, and lime juice. Add the tomato juice and balsamic vinegar and stir to combine. Stir in the oil. Season to taste with salt and pepper, add the chopped cilantro, and refrigerate until well chilled.

Just before serving, stir in the avocado and combined shrimp and crab meat. Sprinkle with the cilantro leaves and serve the soup immediately.

Serves 6

Spiced Meatballs

1 1/4 lb (600 g) finely ground (minced) lean beef or lamb

1 medium onion, grated and drained

2 cloves garlic, crushed

1 1/2 teaspoons dried mint

1/2 teaspoon salt

1/2 teaspoon ground black pepper

1 1/2 teaspoons ground cumin

1/3 teaspoon allspice

1 small egg, well beaten

Canola oil

ACCOMPANIMENTS

1 thinly sliced onion

2 very ripe tomatoes

Plain (natural) yogurt

Sprigs of mint (optional)

In a bowl, combine the ground meat, onion, garlic, mint, salt, pepper, cumin, and allspice. Add the egg and blend thoroughly with your hands, kneading to a smooth consistency. Form into croquette shapes about 2 inches (5 cm) long.

Preheat a grill (barbecue) or broiler (griller). Oil 4 metal skewers. Thread a skewer lengthwise through the meatballs, placing 3 balls on each skewer for main course servings, and 2 for appetizers. Brush with the oil and broil (grill) or grill (barbecue), turning frequently, until cooked through and crisp on the surface.

Separate the onion into rings (if you like, marinate them for a few minutes in a mixture of vinegar, sugar, and salt). Cut the tomatoes in half and squeeze out the seeds; very finely dice the flesh and season lightly with salt and pepper. Serve the meatballs on a warmed platter with the accompaniments. Garnish with the mint sprigs, if desired.

Serves 4

Crab Dip

¼ cup (2 oz/60 g) cream cheese, at room temperature

1 tablespoon mayonnaise

⅓ cup (2 oz/60 g) each finely chopped red and green bell pepper (capsicum)

2 tablespoons finely chopped yellow bell pepper (capsicum)

2 green (spring) onions, finely chopped

1 clove garlic, minced

1 tablespoon lemon juice

Dash of hot-pepper sauce, such as Tabasco

Salt and pepper

½ cup (4 oz/125 g) crabmeat, drained

1 tablespoon chopped fresh dill

Low-Carb Dippers

Fresh vegetables make great dippers. Along with sticks of celery, carrot, and bell peppers (capsicums), try sliced cucumber, uncooked cauliflower and broccoli florets, or sliced mushrooms. Or hollow out cherry tomatoes and fill them with dip. Another popular choice is low-carbohydrate pork rind dippers.

Combine cream cheese, mayonnaise, bell peppers, green onion, and garlic. Stir to combine. Add lemon juice, hot-pepper sauce, and salt and pepper to taste. Mix well. Stir in crabmeat and dill. Allow to stand for 1 hour before serving.

Makes 2 cups (16 oz/500 g)

Guacamole

3 ripe avocados

1 fresh green chili, seeded and finely chopped

1/2 white onion, diced

1/3 cup (1/3 oz/10 g) coarsely chopped cilantro (fresh coriander) leaves

Juice of 1 lime

1/2 teaspoon salt

Ground black pepper

Cut each avocado lengthwise into quarters and remove the pit. Peel off the skin and place the pulp in a bowl. Mash roughly with a fork. Add the remaining ingredients and mix until just combined; chunks of avocado should remain visible. Serve immediately accompanied with vegetable sticks.

Makes about 2 cups (16 oz/500 g)

Tapenade

1 1/2 cups (7 oz/220 g) pitted black olives in brine, such as Niçoise or Kalamata, patted dry

2 oil-packed anchovy fillets, drained

1/4 cup (2 oz/60 g) canned oil-packed tuna, drained (optional)

3 tablespoons capers

1 clove garlic, minced

3 tablespoons extra virgin olive oil

Place the olives in the bowl of a food processor and purée until roughly chopped. Add anchovies, tuna (if using), capers, garlic, and oil. Process for 30 seconds. Store in an airtight container in the refrigerator for up to 1 week.

Makes 1 1/2 cups (12 oz/375 g)

Oysters with Dipping Sauces

36 oysters

LEMON VINAIGRETTE

1/2 cup (4 fl oz/125 ml) olive oil

3 tablespoons lemon juice

2 teaspoons grain mustard

1/2 teaspoon sugar (optional)

HORSERADISH
CREAM SAUCE

1 cup (8 fl oz/250 ml) sour cream

2 tablespoons grated horseradish
or 1 tablespoon cream-style
prepared horseradish

2 tablespoon capers

2 drops hot-pepper sauce, such
as Tabasco

CILANTRO PESTO WITH
LIME AND CHILIS

2 cloves garlic

2 mild green chilis, seeded

1 cup (1 oz/30 g) cilantro
(fresh coriander) leaves, washed
and dried

2 tablespoons lime juice

For the lemon vinaigrette,
combine all the ingredients in
a screw-top jar and shake well.

For the horseradish cream, mix
all the ingredients until well
combined. Refrigerate for at least
2 hours before serving.

For the cilantro pesto, combine
all the ingredients in a food
processor and process until
finely chopped, but still
retaining some texture.
Refrigerate for at least 1 hour
before serving.

Just before serving, shuck the
oysters, taking care not to lose
any of their flavorful juices.
Arrange the oysters in their half-
shells on a large platter. Place
each of the dipping sauces in a
separate small bowl and add to
the platter. Serve immediately.

Serves 3 to 4

Shrimp with Garlic and Baked Tomato

4 tomatoes, about 1 1/2 lb (750 g) total weight

Salt and ground black pepper

1/3 cup (2 1/2 fl oz/80 ml) olive oil

1 lb (500 g) medium-sized shrimp (prawns), peeled and deveined

1 tablespoon minced garlic

1 tablespoon sherry vinegar

2 tablespoons chopped fresh parsley

Dash of cayenne pepper

Preheat an oven to 450°F (220°C/Gas Mark 6).

Cut the tomatoes in half and place them, cut side up, in a shallow baking dish. Season to taste with salt and pepper and drizzle on 2 tablespoons of the olive oil. Bake until the tomatoes are cooked through but still firm, about 15 minutes.

About 3 minutes before the tomatoes are done, in a frying pan over high heat, warm 1 tablespoon of the olive oil.

Add the shrimp and salt and pepper to taste and sauté until the shrimp are pink and firm, 2–3 minutes.

Transfer the baked tomatoes to individual serving dishes. Place the sautéed shrimp on top of the tomatoes, dividing them evenly.

In a small saucepan over high heat, combine the garlic and the remaining 3 tablespoons olive oil, and sauté until the garlic turns golden brown, about 1 minute.

Add the vinegar and deglaze the pan by stirring to dislodge any browned bits from the bottom of the pan, about 30 seconds. Immediately spoon the contents of the saucepan over the shrimp and tomatoes, dividing it evenly among the servings. Sprinkle with the parsley and cayenne pepper. Serve at once.

Serves 4

Pumpkin Soup

1 clove garlic

1 whole clove

1 sprig fresh thyme

4 cups (32 fl oz/1 liter) vegetable stock

1½ lb (750 g) pumpkin flesh, cut into ¾-inch (2-cm) cubes

Salt and ground black pepper

2 pinches grated nutmeg

2 pinches cayenne pepper

⅓ cup (2½ fl oz/80 ml) light (single) cream

Fresh sage leaves, to garnish

Tie the garlic, whole clove, and thyme in a small square of cheesecloth (muslin). Combine the cheesecloth bag, stock, pumpkin, and a pinch of salt in a large saucepan. Bring to a boil, then reduce the heat to low. Cover and cook for 30 minutes, stirring several times during cooking.

Discard the cheesecloth bag. Blend or process the soup until it is very smooth. Return to the pan and reheat, stirring in the salt and pepper, nutmeg, cayenne pepper, and cream.

Serve immediately, garnished with sage leaves.

Serves 4 to 5

Grilled Eggplant and Goat Cheese Rolls

1 eggplant (aubergine)

Olive oil, for brushing

Ground pepper

1/3 cup (1/2 oz/15 g) chopped fresh chives

3 cloves garlic, minced

Balsamic vinegar, for sprinkling

Leaves from 12 fresh thyme sprigs, finely chopped, or 1 tablespoon dried thyme, crumbled

Salt

1 log (7 oz/220 g) fresh goat cheese, at room temperature

Cut off and discard a thin slice from both ends of the eggplant. Cut the eggplant lengthwise into slices 1/4 inch (5 mm) thick.

Prepare a fire in a charcoal grill (barbecue), or preheat a ridged stove-top grill pan until very hot. Brush the eggplant slices lightly on one side with olive oil, then place them, oiled sides down, on the grill in a single layer. Grill (barbecue) until the eggplant begins to soften and the grill marks are clearly visible. Brush the tops with additional oil, turn, and continue grilling for about 4 minutes total, or until soft but not too deeply browned. As the eggplant slices are done, use tongs to transfer them to a large, warmed platter.

Arrange half of the slices in a single layer on another platter and sprinkle with salt and pepper to taste. Scatter half each of the chives and garlic evenly over the slices and sprinkle with a little balsamic vinegar. Sprinkle all the thyme evenly over the top. Top with the remaining eggplant slices, again in a single layer, and scatter the remaining

chives and garlic over the top. Sprinkle with a little more vinegar. Let stand in a cool place for at least 2 hours, or cover and refrigerate for up to 3 days.

When ready to serve, carefully spread each eggplant slice with a portion of the goat cheese and roll into a tight roll. Secure with a toothpick, if desired. Serve at room temperature.

Serves 4 to 6

Haloumi and Vegetable Kabobs

3 tablespoons olive oil

1 tablespoon red wine vinegar

1 small red bell pepper (capsicum)

1 small green bell pepper (capsicum)

1 green zucchini (courgette)

8 oz (250 g) haloumi cheese

8 button mushrooms

½ teaspoon dried chili flakes

Preheat a broiler (griller) to high. Combine oil and vinegar.

Cut the bell peppers, zucchini, and haloumi into 1-inch (2.5-cm) pieces. Cut the mushrooms in halves if they are large. Thread the vegetables and cheese onto skewers. Place in a shallow nonaluminum dish, pour over the oil and vinegar mixture, and sprinkle with chili flakes. Set aside for 10 minutes.

Remove the skewers from marinade, reserving marinade. Transfer the skewers to a broiler tray and broil, turning and brushing with the reserved marinade, for about 10 minutes, or until the vegetables are softened. Serve immediately.

Serves 4

Onion and Herb Frittata

2 tablespoons olive oil

2 onions, chopped

4 eggs

2 oz (60 g) chopped
fresh spinach

2 tablespoons chopped
fresh sage

2 tablespoons chopped
fresh parsley

2 tablespoons chopped
fresh basil

2 tablespoons chopped
fresh oregano

Heat 1 tablespoon of the oil in
a frying pan, add the onions,
and cook over low heat until
softened. Remove the onions
from the pan. Beat the eggs in
a bowl, add the onion, spinach,
and herbs, and mix well.

Heat the remaining oil in an
ovenproof nonstick frying pan;
pour in egg mixture and cook
over medium heat until the base
is golden and the frittata starts
to set. Place the pan under a hot
broiler (griller) and broil until
the top of frittata is set. Remove
the frittata from pan, allow to
cool, cut into wedges, and serve.

Serves 6

Stuffed Field Mushrooms

8 large field or large white mushrooms

4 green (spring) onions, chopped

1 small fresh red chili, seeded and finely chopped

2 oz (60 g) goat cheese, crumbled

1 tablespoon chopped parsley

2 tablespoons extra virgin olive oil

Preheat a broiler (griller) to medium-high. Trim the stems from mushrooms. Chop stems and place in a small bowl. Add the green onion, chili, cheese, parsley, and oil and toss together.

Fill the mushroom caps with the mixture and place on a broiler (griller) tray. Broil until the mushrooms soften and change color. Serve hot.

Serves 4

Vegetable Omelet

1/3 cup (2 1/2 fl oz/80 ml) olive oil

2 cloves garlic, minced

2 eggplants (aubergines) (about 13 oz/410 g total weight), peeled and diced

1 red bell pepper (capsicum) (6 1/2 oz/200 g), finely chopped

2 zucchini (courgettes) (about 13 oz/410 g total weight), peeled and finely chopped

2 large, ripe tomatoes (about 8 oz/250 g total weight), peeled and finely chopped

Salt and ground black pepper

4 eggs

2 tablespoons milk

Heat 3 tablespoons of the oil in a large frying pan. Cook the garlic, then add the eggplant, followed by the bell pepper and zucchini, stirring occasionally. Add the tomatoes, season with salt and pepper to taste, and cook on low heat for 10 minutes. Set aside.

Break the eggs into a bowl, add a little salt and pepper, then pour in the milk and beat well. Add the fried vegetables. Heat the remaining oil in a clean frying pan, pour in the egg and vegetable mixture, and cook the omelet on one side. Turn it out onto a plate or wide lid. Slide it back into the pan and cook the other side. Serve at once.

Serves 4

About Eggplants

Probably originating in India, eggplants (aubergines) have been cultivated for centuries in Southeast Asia, China, and Turkey. They are available in a variety of colors and sizes. Most common is the large, purplish-black type, also known as globe eggplant, that is popular in Mediterranean, Middle Eastern, and Indian cooking. If no particular type is specified, it is safe to assume that globe eggplant is intended. Other varieties range from pale green to yellow and white, and may be round, oval, long and slender, or little bigger than peas.

Choose firm eggplants with smooth, glossy, unblemished skin. They should be heavy for their size. Store uncut eggplants, unwrapped, for up to 2 weeks. They need refrigeration only in hot climates. Cut fruit discolors quickly, due to oxidization, so it is best to cook eggplant as soon as possible after preparation. Any unused cut fruit should be wrapped tightly in plastic wrap. The discoloration is of aesthetic concern only; the discolored part may be cut away and the rest of the eggplant eaten.

Mussels with Cilantro and Tomato

30 small mussels in their shells

3 tomatoes, peeled, seeded, and chopped

Salt and pepper

1 red bell pepper (capsicum), finely chopped

1/3 cup (1/3 oz/10 g) finely chopped cilantro (fresh coriander)

1/4 cup (2 fl oz/60 ml) balsamic vinegar

Scrub the mussels, removing any beards that may still be attached. Steam the mussels until they just open; discard any that remain closed.

Remove one half of each of the mussel shells. Place a teaspoonful of tomato onto each mussel; season with salt and pepper to taste. Sprinkle with bell pepper and cilantro and finish with a small drizzle of balsamic vinegar. Serve the mussels hot or cold.

Serves 4 to 6

Egg and Mushroom Flan

2 tablespoons olive oil

1 lb (500 g) fresh button mushrooms, thinly sliced

2 teaspoons chopped fresh herbs (parsley, oregano, thyme)

Salt and black pepper

4 large eggs

Preheat an oven to 350°F (180°C/Gas Mark 4).

Heat the oil in a frying pan, add the mushrooms and sauté until tender. Process the mushrooms in a blender or food processor to form a smooth paste. Add the herbs, salt, pepper, and eggs and mix to combine. Pour into an oiled quiche mold or pie dish and set in a roasting pan. Add hot water to reach halfway up the sides. Bake for 30 minutes, or until the flan is set.

Serves 4 to 6

Figs and Prosciutto

8 fresh figs (or chunks of melon if figs are unavailable)

12 thin slices prosciutto (about 7 oz/220 g)

5 oz (160 g) baby arugula (rocket)

1 tablespoon olive oil

1 tablespoon balsamic vinegar

Black pepper

Cut each fig into 4 pieces. Cut each slice of prosciutto in half lengthwise, forming 24 "ribbons." Wrap each piece of fig with a ribbon of prosciutto.

Place the arugula on a serving platter and top with the wrapped figs. Drizzle with the oil and vinegar and grind black pepper over the top. Serve immediately.

Serves 4

Wild Mushroom Soup

⅓ cup (2 oz/60 g) pine nuts

½ cup (4 fl oz/125 ml) extra virgin olive oil

1 large yellow onion, finely chopped

3 cloves garlic, minced

10 plum (Roma) tomatoes, chopped

1 lb (500 g) fresh shiitake mushrooms, stems removed, sliced

8 oz (250 g) fresh cremini or white mushrooms, stems removed, sliced

6 cups (48 fl oz/1.5 l) water

1 tablespoon chopped fresh basil

1 tablespoon chopped fresh flat-leaf (Italian) parsley

1 tablespoon chopped fresh rosemary

1 tablespoon chopped fresh thyme

Salt and ground black pepper

Preheat an oven to 350°F (180°C/Gas Mark 4).

Spread the pine nuts over a baking sheet and toast in the oven until golden, 5–8 minutes. Remove from the oven and set aside to cool.

Heat the olive oil in a large saucepan over medium heat. Add the onion and cook, stirring often, until soft and golden, about 5 minutes. Add the garlic, tomatoes, and mushrooms and increase the heat to high. Cook, stirring often, until the mushrooms begin to release their liquid, about 7 minutes.

Stir in the water and herbs and bring the mixture to a boil. Reduce the heat to medium-low and simmer, uncovered, stirring occasionally, until the vegetables are tender, 25–30 minutes. Season to taste with salt and pepper. Serve sprinkled with the pine nuts.

Serves 4 to 6

MAIN COURSE SALADS

Greek-Style Chicken Salad

4 skinless, boneless chicken breast halves (1 lb/500 g total)

1/4 cup (2 fl oz/60 ml) lemon juice

2 tablespoons olive oil plus 1/4 cup (2 fl oz/60 ml) extra

1 tablespoon honey

2 cloves garlic, minced

2 tablespoons chopped fresh rosemary

1 tablespoon grain mustard

1 eggplant (aubergine), thinly sliced

1 bunch (1 1/4 lb/625 g) leaf (English) spinach

2 tomatoes, thinly sliced

1 onion, thinly sliced

1/4 cup (2 oz/60 g) black (Riviera) olives

5 oz (160 g) feta cheese, cubed

1/4 cup (2 fl oz/60 ml) extra virgin olive oil

In a shallow, nonmetallic dish, combine the chicken, lemon juice, 2 tablespoons olive oil, honey, garlic, rosemary, and mustard. Cover and refrigerate for several hours or overnight.

Drain the marinade from the chicken and reserve.

In a frying pan over medium heat, warm the remaining 1/4 cup (2 fl oz/60 ml) olive oil. Add the eggplant in batches and cook until lightly browned and tender. Drain on paper towels.

Add the chicken to the frying pan and cook until well browned and cooked through, 10–15 minutes. Take care not to burn the chicken, as honey causes it to brown quickly.

Remove the chicken from the pan and slice.

Arrange the chicken, eggplant, spinach, tomatoes, onion, olives, and cheese on a serving plate or

in a bowl. Add the reserved
marinade to the pan and bring
to a boil. Allow to cool, then
add the extra olive oil and
spoon it over the chicken and
salad. Serve immediately.

Serves 4

Bon-Bon Chicken Salad

SAUCE

1 1/2 tablespoons sesame paste

1 tablespoon chili oil

3/4 teaspoon sugar

1 tablespoon light soy sauce

1 teaspoon aromatic or apple vinegar

2 tablespoons chicken stock

1/2 chicken, about 1 1/2 lb (750 g)

1–2 teaspoons salt

1 tablespoon Chinese rice wine or dry sherry

1 teaspoon sesame oil

1 tablespoon sesame seeds

8 oz (250 g) shredded cucumber

1 red bell pepper (capsicum), shredded

For the sauce, combine the sesame paste, chili oil, sugar, soy sauce, vinegar, and stock.

Rub the chicken with the salt, wine or sherry, and sesame oil. Bring a large pan of water to a boil, place the chicken on a steaming rack, and steam over medium heat for 18–20 minutes. Remove, drain, and allow to cool. When cool, bone and shred the meat. Set aside.

In a wok or frying pan over low heat, lightly brown the sesame seeds. Remove from the pan and set aside.

Place the cucumber on a serving dish. Arrange the chicken on top and sprinkle with the bell pepper and sesame seeds. Pour the sauce on top and serve.

Serves 4 to 6

Tuna Salad

2 large, firm yellow bell peppers (capsicums)

1/3 cup (2 1/2 fl oz/80 ml) plus 2 tablespoons extra virgin olive oil

Juice of 2 lemons

1 tablespoon chopped fresh oregano or 1 teaspoon dried oregano, crumbled

2 cloves garlic, minced

Salt and ground pepper

4 oz (125 g) small, tender green beans, trimmed

Ice water

2 small, firm zucchini (courgettes), cut in half crosswise, then cut lengthwise into thin strips

8 oz (250 g) tuna fillet, cut into thin slices

Olive oil, for brushing

10 round or pear-shaped cherry tomatoes, halved

1/4 cup (1/3 oz/10 g) thinly sliced fresh basil leaves

2 teaspoons capers, rinsed

Preheat a broiler (griller) or preheat an oven to 450°F (220°C/Gas Mark 6).

Arrange the bell peppers on a baking sheet and place in the broiler or oven. Broil (grill) or bake, turning, until the skin is charred and blistered on all sides.

Alternatively, using tongs or a fork, hold the bell peppers over a gas flame until charred and blistered. Immediately place the peppers in a bowl and cover tightly with plastic wrap. Let them steam until cool, about 15 minutes. Using your fingers, peel off the skin, then pull out and discard the stem and seeds. Cut in half lengthwise and trim away the seeds and tough white ribs. Cut each pepper lengthwise into thin strips.

Preheat a ridged stove-top grill pan until very hot.

In a small bowl, whisk together the 1/3 cup (2 1/2 fl oz/80 ml)

extra virgin olive oil, lemon juice, oregano, garlic, and salt and pepper to taste. Set aside.

Bring a saucepan that is three-fourths full of lightly salted water to a boil. Add the green beans to the boiling water, blanch for 1 minute, then drain and immediately plunge them into the ice water to stop the

cooking and preserve the color. Transfer to a colander to drain well. Set aside.

In a frying pan over medium heat, warm the 2 tablespoons extra virgin olive oil. Add the zucchini and fry, stirring occasionally and regulating the heat so that the strips do not burn, until tender and golden brown, about 5 minutes. Using a slotted spoon, transfer to paper towels to drain briefly.

Lightly brush the tuna slices with olive oil and season to taste with salt and pepper. Place the tuna in the stove-top grill pan and cook, turning once, until firm and cooked through, 3–5 minutes. Remove the tuna from the pan and, when cool enough to handle, gently break into large pieces.

In a large bowl, combine the bell peppers, green beans, zucchini, tomatoes, basil, and capers. Whisk the dressing briefly, then drizzle over. Toss gently to coat the vegetables evenly. Add the tuna and toss again gently to mix. Serve immediately, or cover and refrigerate for up to 24 hours.

Serves 6 to 8

Rare Roast Beef Salad

DRESSING

1/3 cup (2 1/2 fl oz/80 ml) extra virgin olive oil

1/4 cup (2 fl oz/60 ml) lemon juice

2 tablespoons finely chopped chives

1 tablespoon tiny capers

1 tablespoon finely chopped sun-dried bell pepper (capsicum)

Salt and ground black pepper

MUSTARD MAYONNAISE

1/4 cup (2 fl oz/60 ml) mayonnaise

1 tablespoon Dijon mustard

2 teaspoons Worcestershire sauce

Dash of hot-pepper sauce, such as Tabasco

SALAD

12 large slices rare roast beef

6 oz (190 g) cherry tomatoes, halved

1 head (3 1/2 oz/105 g) radicchio, washed and torn

1 bunch (3 1/2 oz/105 g) corn salad (lamb's lettuce/mâche), washed and torn

8 oz (250 g) home-cooked or canned artichoke hearts, halved

1/3 cup (2 1/2 oz/80 g) tiny cornichons (tiny gherkins or dill pickles)

For the dressing, combine all of the dressing ingredients in a small bowl. Whisk until the ingredients are well blended.

For the mustard mayonnaise, combine all of the mayonnaise ingredients in a small bowl and stir well.

Divide the remaining ingredients among 6 serving plates. Spoon the dressing over and place a tablespoon of mayonnaise in the center of each salad. Serve while the salad is still warm.

Serves 6

Chicken, Avocado, and Mango Salad with Curry Macadamia Dressing

DRESSING

3 tablespoons olive oil

1 onion, finely chopped

2 teaspoons curry powder

1 tablespoon mango chutney

1/4 cup (1 oz/30 g) unsalted macadamia nuts

2 tablespoons raspberry vinegar

1/2 cup (4 fl oz/125 ml) mayonnaise

1/4 cup (2 fl oz/60 ml) light (single) cream

4 skinless, boneless, chicken breast halves, poached

1 bunch (3 1/2 oz/105 g) arugula (rocket), washed and stemmed

1 large mango, peeled, pitted, and sliced

2 large avocados, peeled, pitted, and sliced

1 bunch fresh chives, cut into 2-inch (5-cm) lengths

For the dressing, heat 1 tablespoon of the oil over medium heat in a small saucepan. Add the onion and cook until it is translucent. Add the curry powder and cook, stirring, for 1 minute. Remove from the heat and stir in the mango chutney, mixing well. Set aside until cool.

In a blender or food processor, process the macadamia nuts briefly until chopped, add the remaining oil and the vinegar and process until well combined.

Add the macadamia mixture to the cooled onion mixture. Stir in the mayonnaise and cream. Mix well.

Slice the cooked chicken breasts lengthwise into 5–6 strips. Arrange the arugula, chicken, mango, and avocado on individual serving dishes. Spoon some of the dressing onto each serving plate.

Garnish with the chives and serve immediately.

Serves 4

Smoked Ham and Camembert Salad

DRESSING

1/4 cup (1 oz/45 g) shelled pecans

Juice of 1 lemon

1 clove garlic

1/8 teaspoon salt

1/4 cup (2 fl oz/60 ml) olive oil

1/4 cup (2 fl oz/60 ml) sour cream

1 tablespoon finely chopped chives

Grated zest of 1/2 lemon

SALAD

1 head butter (Boston) lettuce, washed and torn

1 1/2 oz (45 g) snow pea (mangetout) sprouts

2 Granny Smith apples, cut into julienne and sprinkled with the juice of 1/2 lemon

6 1/2 oz (200 g) smoked ham, cut into julienne

6 1/2 oz (200 g) Camembert, at room temperature, thinly sliced

2 1/2 oz (80 g) pecans, toasted and roughly chopped

For the dressing, chop the pecans finely in a food processor fitted with a metal blade. Add the lemon juice, garlic, salt, and oil and process until thoroughly combined. Add the sour cream, chives, and lemon zest and combine thoroughly.

Arrange the salad ingredients on a serving platter or individual plates. Spoon the dressing over the salad. Serve immediately.

Serves 3 to 4

Chicken Salad Niçoise

DRESSING

2 x 6-oz (190-g) jars marinated artichoke hearts

2 tablespoons balsamic vinegar

1 tablespoon capers

1 tablespoon anchovy paste

1 tablespoon Dijon mustard

4 cloves garlic, minced

1/2 teaspoon herbes de Provence

SALAD

12 oz (375 g) skinless, boneless chicken breast halves

Spinach or romaine (cos) lettuce

2 tomatoes, cut into wedges

1 green or red bell pepper (capsicum), cut into strips

2 hard-boiled eggs, sliced

1 fresh fennel bulb, sliced

1/4 cup (1 oz/30 g) pitted Niçoise, Kalamata, or other black olives

1/4 cup (1 oz/30 g) chopped walnuts

For the dressing, drain the artichokes, reserving the liquid. In a screw-top jar, combine the reserved artichoke liquid, vinegar, capers, anchovy paste, mustard, garlic, and herbes de Provence. Shake well.

For the salad, in a large, strong plastic bag, combine the chicken and 1/4 cup (2 fl oz/60 ml) of the salad dressing. (Cover and chill remaining salad dressing until serving time.) Seal the bag and turn to coat the chicken with the dressing. Marinate in the refrigerator for 8–24 hours. Drain the marinade from the chicken and discard marinade.

Turn on the broiler (griller). Place chicken on an unheated rack of broiler pan. Broil (grill), 5–6 inches (13–15 cm) from heat, for 6–8 minutes per side, or until cooked through. Cool slightly, then slice each chicken breast diagonally. Line a large serving dish with spinach or lettuce leaves. Arrange chicken, artichokes, tomatoes, bell pepper

strips, eggs, fennel, olives, and
walnuts on the dish and drizzle
with the remaining dressing.
Serve at once.

Serves 4

Chef's Salad

VINAIGRETTE

2 tablespoons lemon juice

2 teaspoons Dijon mustard

1 teaspoon finely minced shallot

Salt and ground pepper

1/4 cup (2 fl oz/60 ml) vegetable oil

2 tablespoons extra virgin olive oil

SALAD

2 heads lettuce, pale inner leaves only, torn into bite-size pieces

5 oz (160 g) honey-baked ham, cut into julienne strips

5 oz (160 g) smoked chicken or roast turkey, cut into julienne strips

8 oz (250 g) Monterey Jack or Swiss cheese, cut into julienne strips

8 red or yellow cherry tomatoes, quartered

3 hard-boiled eggs, quartered

For the vinaigrette, in a small bowl, whisk together the lemon juice, mustard, shallot, and salt and pepper. Slowly pour in the vegetable oil and olive oil, whisking continuously. Whisk until emulsified, 10–20 seconds.

For the salad, place the lettuce in a large bowl or 4 individual bowls. Arrange the ham, chicken or turkey, and cheese on top, keeping each ingredient separate and radiating the strips outward from the center of the bowl. Place the tomato and egg in between the meats and cheese.

Serve the salad with the vinaigrette on the side. Dress and toss at the table.

Serves 4

Thai Beef Salad

BEEF

2 cloves garlic

2 tablespoons finely chopped cilantro (fresh coriander)

1 teaspoon ground black pepper

2 tablespoons soy sauce

1 tablespoon Thai fish sauce

1 tablespoon peanut or corn oil

1 lb (500 g) boneless sirloin steak

VINAIGRETTE AND SALAD

2 cloves garlic, minced

2 small fresh red or green chilis, chopped

1 tablespoon sugar, or equivalent sweetener

1/4 cup (2 fl oz/60 ml) Thai fish sauce

1/3 cup (2 1/2 fl oz/80 ml) lime juice

6 large red-leaf lettuce leaves, torn into pieces

3 small firm tomatoes, cut into wedges

1 small red (Spanish) onion, thinly sliced

1 small cucumber, peeled and thinly sliced

2 tablespoons coarsely chopped cilantro (fresh coriander), plus whole cilantro leaves for garnish

2 tablespoons coarsely chopped fresh mint

To prepare the beef, use a mortar and pestle and combine the garlic, cilantro, and pepper and mash to a paste. Stir in the soy sauce, fish sauce, and oil. Place the beef in a shallow dish and rub the garlic and cilantro mixture over both sides. Marinate for 1 hour at room temperature or cover and refrigerate for up to 4 hours.

To make the vinaigrette, use a mortar and pestle and combine the garlic and chilis and mash to a paste. Stir in the sugar, fish sauce, and lime juice. Set aside.

Preheat a two-sided electric indoor grill (barbecue) or a ridged, stove-top grill pan, according to the manufacturer's instructions.

If you are using the two-sided grill, place the beef on the grill, close the cover, and cook to the desired degree of doneness, 4–5 minutes for medium rare. Set aside to cool.

If you are using the stove-top grill pan, cook the beef to the desired degree of doneness, 8–10 minutes for medium rare, turning it once midway through cooking. Set aside to cool.

To assemble: In a large bowl, toss the salad ingredients together with 2½ tablespoons of the vinaigrette. Thinly slice the beef across the grain, place the slices in a bowl, and toss with the remaining vinaigrette. Divide the salad among 4 plates and mound the beef mixture on top. Garnish with cilantro leaves and serve immediately.

Serves 4

Chicken and Almond Salad

3 skinless, boneless chicken breast halves (12 oz/375 g total)

Salt and pepper

2/3 cup (5 fl oz/155 ml) water

1 butter (Boston) or Bibb (mignonette) lettuce, torn into serving pieces

2 cups (2 oz/60 g) lightly packed watercress sprigs

1/3 cup (2 oz/60 g) toasted almonds, to serve

2 tablespoons grated lemon zest, to serve

LEMON MAYONNAISE

2 eggs

1/3 cup (2 1/2 fl oz/80 ml) lemon juice

2 tablespoons Dijon mustard

1/2 cup (4 fl oz/125 ml) light olive oil

1/4 cup (2 fl oz/60 ml) peanut oil

Grated zest of 2 lemons

Preheat an oven to 300°F (150°C/Gas Mark 2).

Place the chicken in a single layer in a baking dish. Sprinkle the chicken with salt and pepper to taste. Add the water and bake the chicken until it is cooked through, 30 minutes. Remove the chicken from the dish and cut it into strips. Combine with the salad greens in a large bowl.

For the mayonnaise, place the eggs, lemon juice, and mustard in the bowl of a food processor.

Process for 1 minute. Combine the oils and, with the motor running, add the oils in a slow, steady stream. Process until thoroughly combined. Stir in the lemon zest.

Toss the mayonnaise with the greens and chicken and sprinkle with the almonds and lemon zest. Serve soon after preparing.

Serves 6

Goat Cheese, Pancetta, and Asparagus Salad with Vinaigrette

3½ oz (105 g) pancetta, thinly sliced

2 bunches (9 oz/275 g) fresh asparagus spears, halved lengthwise

Salt

1 tablespoon hazelnut oil

3 tablespoons hazelnuts, skins removed

1 head (3½ oz/105 g) butter (Boston) lettuce, washed and torn

1 head (3½ oz/105 g) oakleaf lettuce, washed and torn

5 oz (160 g) goat cheese, sliced or crumbled

DRESSING

2 tablespoons hazelnut oil

1 tablespoon white wine vinegar

1 tablespoon light olive oil

Place the pancetta slices under a broiler (griller) and broil until crisp. Drain on paper towels and break into pieces.

Blanch the asparagus spears in boiling, salted water until just tender. Run the asparagus under cold water, then drain.

Heat the hazelnut oil in a small frying pan. Toss the hazelnuts in the oil and toast until golden.

For the dressing, combine all of the dressing ingredients in a small bowl. Whisk until they are thoroughly combined.

Arrange the lettuces, asparagus, goat cheese, pancetta, and hazelnuts on individual plates. Drizzle on the dressing and serve immediately.

Serves 4

Baked Red Bell Pepper and Salami Salad

3 red bell peppers (capsicums)

3 red (Spanish) onions

2 cloves garlic

1/4 cup (2 fl oz/60 ml) olive oil

4 oz (125 g) spicy Italian salami, roughly chopped

1/2 jar (4 1/2 oz/140 g) artichoke hearts, drained and halved

1/3 cup (3 1/2 oz/105 g) small black olives

2 teaspoons dried oregano

1 tablespoon balsamic vinegar

Halve the bell peppers and remove the seeds and membranes. Cut each half into 4 pieces. Peel the onions and cut each into eighths. Peel and chop the garlic and add to the olive oil.

Preheat an oven to 400°F (200°C/Gas Mark 5).

Arrange the bell pepper slices and onions in a shallow baking dish. Pour on the garlic oil. Bake for 20 minutes.

Remove the baking dish from the oven and stir the bell peppers and onions gently. Add the salami, artichokes, olives, and oregano. Return to the oven for 15 minutes. Remove from the oven and drizzle with the balsamic vinegar.

Serve the salad warm, or at room temperature.

Serves 4 to 6

Spiced Lime Chicken Salad

2 tablespoons vegetable oil

6 skinless, boneless chicken breast halves (1 1/2 lb/750 g total)

1 tablespoon ground cumin

2 carrots

7 oz (220 g) fresh asparagus, chopped

7 oz (220 g) sugar snap peas

1 cup (5 oz/160 g) bean sprouts

1 red bell pepper (capsicum), thinly sliced

1 head romaine (cos) lettuce, torn

1 onion, thinly sliced

DRESSING

3/4 cup (6 fl oz/190 ml) canola oil

1 teaspoon grated lime zest

1/2 cup (4 fl oz/125 ml) lime juice

1/4 cup (1/4 oz/7 g) chopped cilantro (fresh coriander)

2 teaspoons chopped fresh chili

2 tablespoons Thai fish sauce

1/2 tablespoon sugar, or equivalent sweetener

3 cloves garlic, minced

2 tablespoons chopped fresh mint

In a frying pan over medium-high heat, warm the oil. Sprinkle the chicken with cumin, add to the pan, and cook until well browned and cooked through, turning once, 10–15 minutes total. Remove from the pan and cut into thick slices.

With a vegetable peeler, peel the carrots lengthwise into thin strips. Place the carrot peel in a bowl of cold water and let stand until crisp, about 30 minutes. In a small saucepan, boil the asparagus and sugar snap peas until just tender, about 4 minutes. Drain and refresh in ice water. Drain again.

For the dressing, in a screw-top jar, combine the oil, lime zest and juice, cilantro, chili, fish sauce, sugar, garlic, and mint. Shake well.

In a bowl, combine the chicken with the vegetables, sprouts, bell pepper, lettuce, and onion, and toss. Drizzle with the dressing just before serving.

NOTE If you don't have much time, you can buy a cooked chicken and use the meat for this recipe. Make double the amount of dressing and refrigerate until needed. You could use this dressing for any salad.

Serves 6

Antipasto

½ cup (4 fl oz/125 ml) olive oil

1 tablespoon balsamic vinegar

2 tablespoons chopped fresh basil

2 cloves garlic, minced

1½ lb (750 g) chicken breast meat, sliced lengthwise in strips

2 × 6-oz (190-g) jars marinated artichoke hearts

1 cup (3 oz/100 g) button mushrooms

½ cup (4 oz/125 g) black olives

3 oz (100 g) bocconcini (mozzarella balls), drained

12 baby radishes, trimmed

6 whole-grain crispbreads

¼ cup (3 oz/100 g) pesto

In a small bowl, combine ⅓ cup (2½ fl oz/80 ml) of the olive oil with the vinegar, basil, and garlic. Mix well.

In a frying pan over medium-high heat, warm the remaining olive oil. Add the chicken and cook, stirring, until cooked through, 10–15 minutes. Pour ¼ cup (2 fl oz/60 ml) of the oil mixture over the chicken. Cool, then refrigerate for several hours.

In a bowl, combine the artichoke hearts and mushrooms. Pour over the remaining oil mixture. Cover and refrigerate for several hours, so the flavors develop.

Arrange the chicken, artichoke hearts, mushrooms, olives, bocconcini, and radishes on a serving platter. Break the crispbreads into large pieces, spread with the pesto, and serve.

Serves 4 to 6

127

Warm Thai Chicken Salad

CHICKEN AND MARINADE

4 boneless, skinless chicken breast halves (about 1 lb/500 g)

3 tablespoons toasted (Asian) sesame oil

1/4 cup (2 fl oz/60 ml) lemon juice

1/4 teaspoon salt

2 cloves garlic, minced

1/2 tablespoon brown sugar

2 tablespoons finely chopped cilantro (fresh coriander)

DRESSING

1 small red chili (seeds included if desired), finely chopped

1 clove garlic, minced

3 tablespoons extra virgin olive oil

1 tablespoon balsamic vinegar

Juice of 2 limes

1 teaspoon sweet chili sauce

SALAD

1 bunch (14 oz/440 g) mizuna, arugula (rocket), or other salad leaves

1 red bell pepper (capsicum), seeds removed and cut into julienne

1 cucumber, cut into julienne

2 carrots, cut into julienne

6 green (spring) onions, sliced

1 cup (1 oz/30 g) loosely packed cilantro (fresh coriander) sprigs

1 cup (1 oz/30 g) shredded purple basil

3 tablespoons sesame seeds, toasted

Place the chicken breasts between 2 sheets of plastic wrap and, using the flat side of a meat mallet, lightly pound to flatten the meat slightly. Cut each breast lengthwise into 4 strips. Combine all of the marinade ingredients in a shallow nonmetallic bowl and mix well. Add the chicken and toss to coat. Cover with plastic wrap and set aside in the refrigerator overnight, or at room temperature for several hours.

For the dressing, combine all of the dressing ingredients in a small bowl and whisk well.

Divide the salad leaves, bell pepper, cucumber, carrot, green onions, cilantro, and basil evenly among 6 individual serving plates.

Heat the sesame oil in a wok or frying pan until smoking. Stir-fry the chicken until cooked through, about 3 minutes. Divide the chicken among the serving plates. Drizzle on the dressing and sprinkle with the toasted sesame seeds.

Serve immediately, while the chicken is still warm.

Serves 4 to 6

Baby Eggplant Salad

11 oz (345 g) baby eggplants (aubergines)

5 oz (160 g) cherry tomatoes, halved

3 tablespoons olive oil

2 tablespoons red wine vinegar

1 clove garlic, minced

Salt and ground black pepper

DRESSING

1/4 cup (2 fl oz/60 ml) plain (natural) yogurt

1/4 cup (2 fl oz/60 ml) sour cream

1 clove garlic

1/2 teaspoon grated fresh ginger

1/2 teaspoon salt

1/2 teaspoon ground cumin

1 tablespoon finely chopped cilantro (fresh coriander), plus sprigs of cilantro for garnish

Preheat a broiler (griller).

Using a sharp knife, slice the eggplant lengthwise into 3 or 4 segments, leaving the stem section intact. Fan out the slices. Brush with a little oil and broil (grill) on both sides until the eggplant is tender and slightly golden, 3–4 minutes.

Arrange the eggplants and the cherry tomatoes on a serving platter. Combine the olive oil, vinegar, garlic, and salt and pepper in a small bowl. Whisk until well blended. Drizzle over the eggplants and tomatoes and allow to cool to room temperature.

Dressing: Combine all of the dressing ingredients in a bowl and stir until thoroughly blended. Just before serving, spoon some of the dressing over the eggplant and tomatoes. Garnish with fresh cilantro sprigs.

Serves 4 to 6

Warm Chicken and Bell Pepper Salad

⅓ cup (2½ fl oz/80 ml) olive oil

4 skinless, boneless chicken breast halves (1 lb/500 g total)

1 each of red, green, and yellow bell peppers (capsicums)

DRESSING

½ cup (1¾ oz/50 g) walnuts

⅓ cup (2½ fl oz/80 ml) walnut oil

¼ cup (2 fl oz/60 ml) olive oil

¼ cup (2 fl oz/60 ml) lemon juice

1 tablespoon fresh thyme leaves

½ tablespoon honey

In a frying pan over medium-high heat, warm the oil. Add the chicken and cook on both sides until well browned and cooked through, 10–15 minutes total. Remove the chicken from the pan and slice.

Cut the bell peppers into fourths and broil (grill), skin side up, until the skin blisters and blackens. Peel and slice thickly.

For the dressing, in a saucepan over low heat, combine all of the ingredients and stir until the honey has dissolved.

Arrange the chicken and bell peppers on plates and sprinkle with salt and pepper. Drizzle with dressing and serve warm.

Serves 4

Spring Vegetable Salad

4 oz (125 g) small green beans

1 bunch asparagus, trimmed

8 oz (250 g) small yellow squash

4 oz (125 g) baby corn

3 1/2 oz (105 g) snow peas
(mangetouts)

1 yellow bell pepper (capsicum),
halved, seeded, and cut into
thick strips

1 red bell pepper (capsicum),
halved, seeded, and cut into
thick strips

12 baby carrots

2 tablespoons extra virgin
olive oil

1/2 teaspoon salt

DRESSING

13 oz (410 g) tomatoes, peeled,
seeded, and finely chopped

1 Spanish (red) onion, finely
chopped

1 clove garlic, minced

1/4 cup (1/4 oz/7 g) shredded
fresh basil

1/2 teaspoon salt

Ground black pepper

2 tablespoons red wine vinegar

1/4 cup (2 fl oz/60 ml) olive oil

For the dressing, combine all
of the dressing ingredients in
a bowl and stir thoroughly. Set
aside for 30 minutes to allow
the flavors to develop.

Bring a large saucepan of water
to a boil. Blanch each of the
vegetables, one at a time, until
just tender, 1–2 minutes each.
Plunge each batch into ice water
as it is removed from the water,
to stop further cooking. Quarter
the squash after blanching.

Combine the vegetables in a
large bowl, add the extra virgin
olive oil and salt, and toss well.

Just before serving, pour the
dressing over the salad and
toss thoroughly.

Serves 4

Stuffed Tomato Salad

8 ripe tomatoes, about 2 lb (1 kg)

1 yellow bell pepper (capsicum), broiled (grilled), peeled, and cut into strips

3 teaspoons capers, rinsed and dried

12 green olives, pitted and chopped

2 oz (60 g) oil-packed sun-dried tomatoes, drained and sliced

6 oz (190 g) artichoke hearts, chopped

6 oz (190 g) oil-packed tuna, drained and flaked

2 tablespoons finely chopped flat-leaf (Italian) parsley

Ground black pepper

2 teaspoons balsamic vinegar

1/4 cup (2 fl oz/60 ml) extra virgin olive oil

Plunge the tomatoes into boiling water for 10 seconds. Drain and peel. Cut the tops off the tomatoes to make "lids." Remove the seeds and pulp from the tomatoes and turn them upside down on paper towels to drain.

In a large bowl, combine the bell pepper, capers, olives, sun-dried tomatoes, artichokes, tuna, parsley, and black pepper. Mix well. Divide among the 4 bottom halves of the tomatoes.

Combine the oil and vinegar and drizzle over the tomatoes. Top with the lids and serve the salad immediately.

Serves 4

MEAT, POULTRY, AND SEAFOOD

Lamb Shoulder with Garlic and Thyme

3 tablespoons olive oil

2 lb (1 kg) boneless lamb shoulder, trimmed of fat and cut into 1-inch (2.5-cm) cubes

1/2 cup (2 1/2 oz/80 g) chopped white onion

1 small carrot, peeled and diced

1 head garlic, separated into cloves and peeled

Salt and ground black pepper

1 tomato, coarsely chopped

1 tablespoon finely chopped fresh thyme

1 cup (8 fl oz/250 ml) dry white wine

3 cups (24 fl oz/750 ml) veal or beef stock

Heat 2 tablespoons of the olive oil in a large frying pan over high heat. Working in batches, add the lamb and cook for about 5 minutes, or until the meat begins to brown. Using a slotted spoon, transfer the meat to a plate and set aside.

Pour off the fat from the pan and increase heat to medium-high. Add the remaining oil and cook the onion, carrot, and garlic for 4–5 minutes, or until the vegetables begin to brown.

Return the lamb to the pan and add 1 teaspoon salt, 1/4 teaspoon pepper, the tomato, thyme, and wine. Reduce the heat to medium and cook for about 5 minutes, or until the liquid is reduced by half. Add the veal stock and bring to a boil over high heat. Reduce the heat to medium and simmer for about 45 minutes, or until the lamb is tender when pierced with a fork.

Pour the contents of the frying pan through a fine-mesh sieve into a clean container. Remove the meat from the sieve, set aside, and keep warm.

Place the vegetables and all of the strained liquid into a food processor fitted with a metal blade, or a blender, and process or blend on high speed for about 30 seconds, or until the sauce is smooth.

Pour the sauce into a saucepan and reheat over medium heat. Adjust the seasoning to taste, if necessary, with salt and pepper. Divide the lamb among warmed serving plates and pour a little of the sauce over. Serve any extra sauce separately.

Serves 4

Butterflied Citrus Chicken

MARINADE

1/3 cup (2½ fl oz/80 ml) olive oil

1/3 cup (2½ fl oz/80 ml) fresh orange juice

1/4 cup (2 fl oz/60 ml) fresh lemon juice

1½ teaspoons dried rosemary, crushed

2 cloves garlic, minced

Salt and pepper to taste

1 whole chicken, 2½–3 lb (1.25–1.5 kg), butterflied

For the marinade, in a small bowl, stir together the oil, orange juice, lemon juice, rosemary, garlic, and salt and pepper. Pour the marinade into a large, strong plastic bag. Add the chicken and seal the bag. Turn the bag to coat the chicken with the marinade. Place in the refrigerator and marinate for 8–24 hours, turning the bag occasionally to evenly coat the chicken. Drain the marinade from the chicken, reserving the marinade.

Heat a covered grill (barbecue) to medium-hot. Place the chicken on the grill rack, skin side up.

Brush with some of the reserved marinade. Cover and cook for 30 minutes. Brush with additional marinade. Cover and cook until cooked through, 30–40 minutes more. Discard any remaining marinade. Or, if you don't have a covered grill (barbecue), cook on an open grill (barbecue) over medium-hot coals, but baste with the marinade about every 10 minutes to prevent the meat from drying out.

Transfer chicken to a platter and serve with roast vegetables or salad, if desired.

Serves 4

Sesame Salmon Steaks

1/3 cup (1 oz/30 g) sesame seeds

1 teaspoon salt

4 salmon steaks, about 1 inch (2.5 cm) thick, center bones removed

In a small saucepan or frying pan, toast the sesame seeds over low heat, stirring constantly, until golden and fragrant, about 4 minutes. Stir in the salt, then transfer them to a plate to cool.

Preheat a two-sided electric indoor grill (barbecue) or ridged grill pan according to the manufacturer's instructions.

Dip both sides of each salmon steak in the sesame seed mixture to coat.

If you are using the two-sided grill, place the fish on the grill, close the cover, and cook until the salmon is barely opaque in the center, 4–5 minutes.

If you are using the grill pan, cook the salmon until it is barely opaque in the center, 8–10 minutes, turning once midway through cooking.

Transfer the salmon to a dish and serve.

Serves 4

Grilled Sesame Chicken

FOR THE MARINADE

2 tablespoons toasted sesame oil

1 tablespoon Chinese rice wine or dry sherry

1 tablespoon rice wine vinegar

1 teaspoon soy sauce

1 teaspoon minced garlic

1 teaspoon minced fresh ginger

FOR THE CHICKEN

4 boneless, skinless chicken breast halves, about 1 lb (500 g)

2 teaspoons sesame seeds

To make the marinade, in a small bowl whisk together all the marinade ingredients.

Place the chicken breasts in a resealable plastic bag and add the marinade. Seal the bag and marinate for 1–8 hours in the refrigerator, turning occasionally.

In a 350°F (180°C/Gas Mark 4) oven or in a frying pan over medium-high heat, toast the sesame seeds until golden and fragrant, 2–3 minutes. Transfer to a small plate to cool.

Preheat a two-sided electric indoor grill (barbecue) or ridged grill pan according to the manufacturer's instructions.

Remove the chicken from the marinade, shaking off the excess.

If you are using the two-sided grill, place the chicken on the grill, close the cover, and cook until the chicken is browned and opaque in the center, about 4–5 minutes.

If you are using the grill pan, cook the chicken until it is browned and opaque in the center, 8–10 minutes, turning it once midway through cooking.

Sprinkle the chicken with sesame seeds, cut the chicken breasts into thin slices, and serve.

Serves 4

Pork with Crunchy Red Cabbage

8 oz (250 g) red cabbage

6 oz (190 g) red (Spanish) onion

1 red apple

4 thin, lean pork chops, about 1½ lb (750 g) total weight

¼ cup (2 fl oz/60 ml) balsamic vinegar

3 tablespoons chopped fresh herbs, such as parsley and/or sage

2 tablespoons fresh lemon juice

Salt and ground black pepper

1 tablespoon canola oil

1 clove garlic, chopped

Finely shred the cabbage. Slice the onion and apples. Trim the pork and make criss-cross cuts on one side. In a small bowl, combine half of the balsamic vinegar, all of the chopped herbs, half of the lemon juice, and salt and pepper to taste.

Warm the oil in a large frying pan over medium heat. Add the onions and garlic and sauté for 2 minutes. Add the cabbage, apple, the remaining vinegar and lemon juice, and salt and pepper to taste. Cook until the liquid has evaporated, about 4–5 minutes; keep warm.

Meanwhile, in a broiler (griller), cook the pork chops for about 4–5 minutes on each side, basting with the lemon mixture. Serve the pork with the warm cabbage.

Serves 4

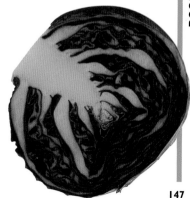

147

Grilled Swordfish Kabobs

1/2 cup (4 fl oz/125 ml) olive oil

6 tablespoons (3 fl oz/100 ml) fresh lemon juice

1 teaspoon paprika

2 bay leaves, crushed, plus 12 whole bay leaves

2 lb (1 kg) swordfish fillets, cut into 1 1/4-inch (3-cm) cubes

2 lemons, thinly sliced, plus lemon wedges for serving

2 green bell peppers (capsicums), seeded, deribbed, and cut into 1 1/4-inch (3-cm) squares

16 ripe but firm cherry tomatoes

Salt and ground black pepper

In a shallow nonaluminum bowl, whisk together the olive oil, lemon juice, paprika, and crushed bay leaves. Add the swordfish cubes, turning to coat well. Cover and marinate in the refrigerator for about 4 hours.

Prepare a fire in a charcoal grill (barbecue) or preheat a broiler (griller).

Remove the fish cubes from the marinade, reserving the marinade.

Thread the fish cubes onto oiled metal skewers, alternating them with the whole bay leaves, lemon slices, bell pepper, and the cherry tomatoes. Sprinkle with salt and pepper.

Place the kabobs on an oiled grill (barbecue) rack or a broiler (griller) pan and grill or broil, turning as needed, and basting a few times with the reserved marinade, until the fish is opaque throughout, about 10 minutes. Discard any unused marinade.

Transfer the kabobs to a warmed platter and serve hot, accompanied with lemon wedges.

Serves 4

Mediterranean Scallop Stew

1½ lb (750 g) bay or sea scallops, with roe if desired

2 tablespoons extra virgin olive oil

1⅓ cups (4 oz/125 g) sliced leeks (white parts only)

½ cup (2 oz/60 g) thinly sliced red (Spanish) onion

6 oz (190 g) pancetta, fat trimmed, cut into thin strips

4 cloves garlic, thinly sliced

2 cups (12 oz/375 g) peeled, seeded, and chopped plum (Roma) tomatoes (fresh or canned)

1½ cups (12 fl oz/375 ml) fruity Italian white wine

5 cups (40 fl oz/1.25 l) fish stock

8 oz (250 g) fresh white mushrooms, stems discarded, sliced

4 tablespoons chopped fresh parsley

1 bay leaf

2 strips orange zest, each 2 inches (5 cm) long and ½ inch (1 cm) wide

½ teaspoon fresh thyme leaves

¼ teaspoon fennel seeds

⅛ teaspoon ground saffron

Salt and ground white pepper

Small fresh basil leaves, for garnishing

Grated Parmesan cheese, for garnishing

If using sea scallops, cut crosswise into ½-inch (1-cm) thick slices. If using bay scallops, leave them whole. Set aside.

Heat the 2 tablespoons olive oil in a large saucepan or stockpot over medium heat.

Add the leeks and onion and cook, stirring, until barely translucent, about 3 minutes; do not allow to brown. Add the pancetta and cook, stirring, for 2 minutes. Stir in the sliced garlic and tomatoes and cook for 1 minute.

Increase the heat to high, add 1¼ cups (10 fl oz/300 ml) of the wine, and stir to dislodge any browned bits on the base of the pan. Bring to a boil, then stir in the stock, mushrooms, parsley, bay leaf, orange zest, thyme, fennel seeds, and saffron. Return to a boil, then reduce heat to medium and simmer, uncovered, for 15–20 minutes, or until the mushrooms are cooked and the liquid has reduced and thickened slightly.

Add the scallops and cook until they are almost opaque in the center, 2–3 minutes. Add the remaining wine and simmer until the scallops are just opaque, about 1 minute longer. Remove the bay leaf and season with salt and pepper to taste.

Serve immediately, garnished with the basil leaves and Parmesan cheese.

Serves 4

Coriander-Crusted Beef Tenderloin with Grilled Green Onions

GREEN ONIONS

¼ cup (2 fl oz/60 ml) fresh lime juice

2 tablespoons soy sauce

2 tablespoons canola oil

1 jalapeño chili, seeded and minced

1 teaspoon grated fresh ginger

16 green (spring) onions, trimmed to about 8 inches (20 cm)

BEEF

1 tablespoon coriander seeds

1½ teaspoons black peppercorns

1½ teaspoons coarse (kosher) salt

4 beef tenderloin (fillet) steaks, cut 1–1¼ inches (2.5–3 cm) thick, about 1–1½ pounds (500–750 g) total

2 teaspoons toasted sesame oil

½ lime

4 teaspoons very coarsely chopped cilantro (fresh coriander)

To prepare the green onions, in a shallow, nonreactive dish, whisk the lime juice, soy sauce, oil, jalapeño, and ginger together. Add the green onions and turn to coat. Let stand at room temperature for about 1 hour.

In a spice grinder, pulse the coriander seeds and peppercorns until coarsely cracked (or put them in a plastic bag and crack them with a rolling pin or heavy pan). Transfer to a small dish and mix in the salt. Rub the steaks on both sides with the sesame oil, then coat them with the spice mixture.

Preheat a two-sided electric indoor grill (barbecue) or ridged grill pan according to the manufacturer's instructions.

If you are using the two-sided grill, arrange the green onions on the grill, close the cover, and cook until they are browned and tender (turning if necessary to make grill marks on both sides), 8–10 minutes. Set the onions aside and keep them warm.

Place the steaks on the grill, close the cover, and cook to the desired degree of doneness, 4–5 minutes for medium rare. Transfer the steaks to a cutting board and let stand for 5 minutes.

If you are using the grill pan, cook the green onions until they are browned and tender, about 15 minutes, turning them once midway through cooking. Set aside and keep them warm.

Cook the steaks to the desired degree of doneness, 8–10 minutes for medium rare, turning them once midway through cooking. Transfer to a cutting board and let stand for 5 minutes.

Cut the steaks into 1/2-inch (1-cm) thick slices and squeeze the lime half over the meat. Fan the slices onto 4 serving plates and sprinkle with cilantro. Arrange the green onions next to the steaks and serve at once.

Serves 4

Lamb in Honey Sauce

8 oz (250 g) lean boneless lamb

1/2 tablespoon cornstarch (cornflour)

1 tablespoon hoisin sauce

1/2 teaspoon sesame oil

3 tablespoons peanut oil

SEASONINGS

1 tablespoon light soy sauce

1 teaspoon brown vinegar

1 teaspoon Chinese rice wine or dry sherry

1 teaspoon ginger juice (use a garlic press)

1 teaspoon honey

1 teaspoon sugar

1/2 teaspoon cornstarch (cornflour)

Slice the lamb across the grain into thin slices.

Place the lamb in a dish. Dust with the cornstarch to coat the meat pieces evenly. Add the hoisin sauce and sesame oil, and mix well.

Preheat a wok or large frying pan. Add the peanut oil and heat until medium-hot. Add the lamb and stir-fry for 1–2 minutes,

stirring with chopsticks to separate the slices. Remove and drain well. Pour off all but 1 tablespoon of the oil and stir in all the seasoning ingredients. Bring to a boil. Return the lamb to the wok and stir quickly over high heat until the sauce coats the lamb slices. Serve at once.

Serves 4

Drunken Pork with Cabbage and Pears

Bouquet garni

2 white onions, diced

2 carrots, peeled and diced

2 stalks celery, diced

3 cloves garlic

30 whole black peppercorns

5 cups (40 fl oz/1.25 l) dry red wine, such as Cabernet or Merlot

Salt to taste, plus 1 tablespoon extra

3 lb (1.5 kg) boneless pork shoulder, cut into 1-inch (2.5-cm) cubes

6 tablespoons (3 fl oz/100 ml) olive oil

4 cups (32 fl oz/1 liter) veal or chicken stock

1 head green cabbage, thinly sliced

3 tablespoons (1½ oz/45 g) unsalted butter

¼ vanilla bean, split in half lengthwise

3 ripe but firm pears, such as Comice, cored, peeled, and cut into ¾-inch (2-cm) cubes

½ cup (½ oz/15 g) chopped fresh parsley

In a large, shallow, nonreactive dish, combine the bouquet garni, onions, carrots, celery, garlic, peppercorns, all but 1/2 cup (4 fl oz/125 ml) of the red wine, and salt to taste. Stir to mix. Add the pork and turn to coat evenly. Cover and refrigerate in the marinade overnight, or for at least 5 hours.

Drain the meat and vegetables in a sieve, reserving marinade in a small saucepan. Bring marinade to a boil, then remove from the heat and set aside. Separate the meat from the vegetables.

Warm 2 tablespoons of olive oil in a frying pan on high heat. Pat the meat dry with paper towels.

Working in small batches and adding more oil as needed, cook the meat for about 2 minutes, browning on all sides. Transfer the meat to a large saucepan.

Add the reserved vegetables to the same frying pan and cook over medium-high heat for about 5 minutes, or until they begin to brown. Transfer the vegetables to the saucepan with the meat, along with the reserved marinade.

Bring to a boil over high heat and boil for about 10 minutes, or until reduced by half. Add the veal stock and return to a boil. Reduce heat to medium and simmer, uncovered, for

50–60 minutes, or until the pork is tender.

Meanwhile, fill another large saucepan two-thirds full with water, add the 1 tablespoon salt, and bring to a boil. Add the cabbage, return to a boil, and cook for about 2 minutes, or until wilted.

Drain the cabbage, rinse with cold water to refresh; drain again.

Melt the butter in a clean frying pan over medium heat. Add the cabbage and cook for 2 minutes. Remove from heat and set aside.

In another small frying pan, combine the reserved ½ cup (4 fl oz/125 ml) red wine, the

vanilla bean, and the pears and bring to a boil. Reduce the heat to medium and simmer, turning the fruit every few minutes, for 5–10 minutes, or until tender.

Drain the meat and vegetables in a sieve, reserving the juices. Cover the juices to keep them warm. Separate the pork from the vegetables; discard the vegetables.

Arrange a bed of cabbage on a warmed platter. Place the pork on top of the cabbage, and pour the reserved juices over the top. Scatter the poached pear cubes around the meat. Garnish with parsley and serve at once.

Serves 6

Recipe Variations Red cabbage can be substituted in this recipe and prepared in the same way as green cabbage. Or, for a Hungarian touch, use canned sauerkraut. The sharpness of the sauerkraut is a good foil to the richness of the pork. Warm the sauerkraut, drain well, and arrange on a warmed platter. Place the pork on top and serve.

Firecracker Chicken Thighs

1 1/2–2 lb (750 g–1 kg) skinless chicken thighs

2–3 tablespoons hot bean paste

2 tablespoons soy sauce

2 tablespoons toasted sesame seeds, crushed

1 tablespoon sesame oil

1/2 tablespoon sugar

1/4 cup (3/4 oz/20 g) minced green (spring) onions

4 large cloves garlic, minced (about 1 tablespoon)

Salt and pepper to taste

Steamed bok choy, to serve (optional)

Grilled eggplant, to serve (optional)

Score the chicken thighs on both sides by making shallow diagonal cuts about 1 inch (2.5 cm) apart.

In a large mixing bowl, stir together the bean paste, soy sauce, sesame seeds, sesame oil, sugar, green onions, garlic, and salt and pepper. Pour the mixture into a strong plastic bag. Add the chicken pieces. Seal the bag and turn it to coat the chicken evenly. Marinate in the refrigerator for 4–24 hours, turning from time to time. Drain, reserving the marinade.

Heat a grill (barbecue) to medium heat. Place the chicken on the cooking rack and grill (barbecue) for 15 minutes, then turn and cook for a further 10–15 minutes. Baste both sides of the meat with the reserved marinade and grill until the chicken is cooked through, about 5 minutes more, turning once. Discard any remaining marinade. Serve with steamed bok choy and grilled eggplant, if desired.

Serves 4 to 6

Grilled Stuffed Leg of Lamb

1 leg of lamb, about 5 lb (2.5 kg)

Salt and ground black pepper

6 oz (190 g) ground (minced) pork

6 oz (190 g) ground (minced) veal

4 oz (125 g) cooked ham, finely ground (minced)

4 oz (125 g) chicken livers, very finely chopped, or pâté

2 tablespoons (1 oz/30 g) olive oil

1 small onion, finely chopped

3 oz (100 g) fresh mushrooms, finely chopped

1 teaspoon dried mixed Provençal or Italian herbs

Salt and ground pepper

10 small sprigs rosemary

2 cloves garlic, slivered

Preheat a covered grill (barbecue) to medium, or preheat an oven to 350°F (180°C/Gas Mark 4).

Remove the lamb bone by cutting the length of the leg on the thinnest side, where the bone is close to the surface. Use a small sharp knife to work around the bone until it can be removed (or ask your butcher to bone the leg). Season the inside surface with salt and pepper.

Mix the ground meats with the ham and chicken liver or pâté. Heat the olive oil in a frying pan and cook the onion until slightly softened and lightly colored. Add the mushrooms and cook for 2–3 minutes. Add the dried herbs and salt and pepper, and mix the contents of the pan with the meats. Knead the stuffing t o combine the ingredients well.

Spread the stuffing over the inside of the lamb leg and fold the meat around the stuffing, forming it back into its original shape. Tie it securely at close intervals with kitchen string. Rub with salt and pepper, pierce in several places with a sharp knife, and insert a small sprig of rosemary and a sliver of garlic in each slit. Roast in the grill (barbecue) or the oven for about 1 1/2 hours, or until cooked through. Baste the meat from time to time during cooking with its own juices. Remove and allow to rest in a warm place for 10 minutes before slicing to serve.

Serves 6

Meat, Poultry, and Seafood

Mustard Steaks

2 x 6-oz (190-g) sirloin or tenderloin (fillet) steaks, about ½ inch (1 cm) thick

Canola oil

2 small golden (French) shallots, finely chopped

2 cloves garlic, minced

Salt and ground black pepper

⅓ cup (2½ fl oz/80 ml) light (single) cream

¼ cup (2 fl oz/60 ml) brandy

1 tablespoon Dijon mustard

3 oz (100 g) mixed mushrooms

¼ cup (2 fl oz/60 ml) water

Thin slices of French bread, to serve (optional)

Trim the steaks and lightly score the flesh with a knife.

Brush a little oil over a small, heavy based frying pan. Heat the pan and, when it is very hot, fry the steaks, allowing 1 minute each side for medium rare, 3 minutes each side for medium, and 4 minutes for well done.

Place the steaks on heated plates and keep them warm in a low oven while you make the sauce.

Cool the frying pan slightly, then add the shallots, garlic, salt and pepper to taste, cream, brandy, mustard, mushrooms, and water. Bring just to a boil, stirring occasionally. Reduce the heat and allow the liquid to bubble until slightly reduced and thickened.

Serve the steaks on slices of French bread, if desired. Spoon a little of the sauce over the steaks. Serve the remaining sauce separately.

Serves 2

Lemon Sole with Salsa Verde

SALSA VERDE

2 bunches of fresh basil (about 2 large handfuls), chopped

2 cloves garlic, minced

4 oz (125 g) grated Parmesan cheese

4 hard-boiled eggs, chopped

Olive oil

Salt and pepper

12 lemon sole fillets, skinned

Flat-leaf (Italian) parsley, to garnish

Preheat a broiler (griller).

For the salsa verde, mix together the basil, garlic, Parmesan, and eggs. Add enough oil so that the mixture is moist yet still stiff enough to hold its shape. Add salt and pepper to taste.

Spread each sole fillet out on a board. Season with salt and pepper, brush with oil, and broil (grill), turning once, until cooked, 8–10 minutes.

To serve, place 2 of the fillets on each of 6 warmed serving plates. With 2 spoons, make lozenge shapes with the salsa verde and arrange beside the fish. Garnish with parsley and serve at once.

Serves 6

Beef Rolls with Blue Cheese Sauce

8 thin beef or veal steaks (about 1 1/4 lb/600 g in total)

8 spears fresh asparagus, trimmed to even lengths

8 thin slices ham or prosciutto

1 tablespoon olive oil

BLUE CHEESE SAUCE

2 tablespoons (1 oz/30 g) butter

1 1/2 tablespoons all-purpose (plain) flour

1/4 cup (2 fl oz/60 ml) dry white wine

1/2 cup (4 fl oz/125 ml) beef stock

1/2 cup (4 fl oz/125 ml) milk

3/4 cup (3 oz/100 g) blue cheese

1/4 cup (1 oz/30 g) grated Cheddar cheese

Salt and ground white pepper

Preheat a broiler (griller).

Place the steaks between 2 sheets of plastic wrap and pound them lightly with the flat side of a meat mallet, until evenly thick.

Parboil the asparagus in lightly salted water for 3 minutes. Drain, refresh under cold, running water, and drain again.

Place a slice of ham or prosciutto and an asparagus spear on each steak. Roll up the steak, secure with toothpicks, and brush with oil. Broil (grill), turning frequently, until the meat is done to your liking.

Meanwhile, for the cheese sauce, melt the butter in a small pan over medium heat, add the flour, and cook, stirring, for 1–2 minutes. Stir in the wine, stock, and milk, increase the temperature, and boil, stirring continuously, until thickened. Add the cheeses and salt and pepper to taste and cook over medium heat until the cheeses melt and the sauce is creamy.

Arrange the rolls on warmed plates and pour on the sauce.

Serves 4

Chicken Rouladen

4 skinless, boneless chicken breast halves (about 1 lb/500 g)

4 teaspoons honey mustard or Dijon mustard

4 slices thinly sliced cooked ham (about 1 1/2 oz/45 g)

1 x 7 1/4-oz (225-g) jar roasted red bell peppers (capsicums), drained and halved

1 tablespoon canola oil

1/2 cup (4 fl oz/125 ml) chicken stock

1/2 cup (4 fl oz/125 ml) dry white wine

2 tablespoons tomato paste

1 tablespoon chopped fresh basil or 1/2 teaspoon dried basil, crushed

1 tablespoon cornstarch (cornflour), mixed with 1 tablespoon water

Place each chicken breast half between 2 pieces of plastic wrap. Using the flat side of a meat mallet, and working from the center to the edges, lightly pound each piece to a 1/4-inch (5-mm) thickness. Remove the plastic wrap.

Spread each piece of chicken with 1 teaspoon of the mustard. Place a slice of ham on each piece of chicken, then a bell pepper half. Fold in the ends of the chicken pieces then roll up, jelly-roll (Swiss-roll) style. Secure with toothpicks.

In a large, heavy based frying pan over medium heat, warm the oil. Add the chicken rolls and brown on all sides. Add the stock and wine and bring to a boil. Reduce heat, cover, and simmer until the chicken is cooked through, about 30 minutes. Remove chicken from the pan and keep warm.

Stir the tomato paste and basil into the pan juices. Stir the cornstarch mixture into the pan. Cook, stirring, until the liquid thickens and bubbles, then continue cooking for a further 1–2 minutes.

With a sharp knife, slice each roll into ¹/₂-inch (1-cm) slices and divide between warmed serving plates. Spoon the sauce over. Serve immediately.

Serves 4

Beef and Ginger Stir-Fry

6 oz (190 g) beef tenderloin (fillet), thinly sliced

MARINADE

1 tablespoon light soy sauce

1 teaspoon sugar

1 tablespoon peanut oil

SAUCE

1 tablespoon light soy sauce

1 tablespoon oyster sauce

1/2 cup (4 fl oz/125 ml) chicken stock

2 teaspoons cornstarch (cornflour)

1 teaspoon Chinese rice wine

1 cup (8 fl oz/250 ml) peanut oil

6–8 slices fresh ginger, each 1/8 inch (3 mm) thick, thinly shredded

3 green (spring) onions, cut into 2-inch (5-cm) lengths

For the marinade, combine the soy sauce, sugar, and peanut oil in a bowl. Add the beef and turn to coat well. Marinate for 15 minutes.

For the sauce, in a separate bowl, combine the soy sauce, oyster sauce, chicken stock, cornstarch, and rice wine. Mix well to combine.

Heat the oil in a wok or frying pan. Add the beef and its marinade and fry for 5 seconds, stirring with chopsticks to separate the slices. Remove the beef, drain, and set aside.

Drain all but 1–2 tablespoons of oil from the wok and reheat. Add the ginger and green onions and stir-fry for 10 seconds. Return the beef to the wok and add the sauce. Bring to a boil. Transfer immediately to a warmed platter and serve.

Serves 2 to 4

Lamb Stew with Artichokes

3–4 tablespoons olive oil

2½ lb (1.25 kg) boneless lamb shoulder, trimmed of excess fat and cut into 2-inch (5-cm) pieces

3 onions, chopped

3 cloves garlic, minced

1½ cups (12 fl oz/375 ml) water or chicken stock, or as needed

½ cup (4 fl oz/125 ml) fresh lemon juice

6 medium artichokes

2 lb (1 kg) assorted greens, such as romaine (cos) lettuce, dandelion greens, or Swiss chard (silverbeet), stems removed, well rinsed, drained, and torn into bite-size pieces (optional)

Salt and ground black pepper

½ cup (½ oz/15 g) chopped fresh dill

2 eggs, at room temperature

Heat 2 tablespoons of olive oil in a large frying pan over high heat. Add the lamb and cook, in batches, for about 10 minutes, or until browned on all sides. Use a slotted spoon to transfer the browned lamb to a large, heavy saucepan.

Add more olive oil, if needed, to the frying pan and cook the onions over medium heat for about 5 minutes, or until softened. Add the garlic and cook for 3 minutes longer. Transfer the contents of the frying pan to the pan containing the lamb. Increase the heat to high, pour ½ cup (4 fl oz/125 ml) of the water or stock into the pan, and deglaze by stirring to dislodge any browned bits from the bottom of the pan. Add the pan juices to the lamb.

Add the remaining 1 cup (8 fl oz/ 250 ml) water or stock to the pan, or as needed to cover the meat. Bring to a boil, reduce the heat to low, cover, and simmer for 45 minutes.

Meanwhile, fill a large bowl three-fourths full with water and add half the lemon juice.

Snap off the tough outer leaves from the artichokes. Using a paring knife, trim the dark green parts from the base and remove the stems. Cut the artichokes lengthwise into fourths, then scoop out and discard the prickly chokes. As they are cut, drop the artichokes into the bowl of acidulated lemon water to prevent them from discoloring. Drain when needed.

If using the greens, fill a large saucepan three-fourths full with water and bring to a boil. Add salt and then the greens. Boil until just tender, 3–5 minutes, then drain well.

When the lamb has simmered for 45 minutes, drain the artichokes and add them to the pan. Continue to simmer for about 15 minutes longer, add the greens, and cook until the lamb and artichokes are tender.

Add the dill and season to taste with salt and pepper. Simmer for 5 minutes. At the last minute, beat the eggs in a bowl until very frothy. Gradually beat in the remaining lemon juice. Then gradually beat in about 1 cup (8 fl oz/250 ml) of the hot lamb juices, beating constantly to prevent curdling. Slowly stir the egg mixture into the hot stew. Heat through but do not allow the stew to boil.

Transfer to a warmed serving dish and serve hot.

Serves 4

Trout Wrapped in Ham

4 freshwater trout, cleaned, with heads intact, each about ¾ lb (375 g)

Salt and ground black pepper

8 thin slices cured ham, such as serrano or prosciutto

⅓ cup (2½ fl oz/80 ml) olive oil

All-purpose (plain) flour, for dusting

Lemon halves, to serve

Sprinkle the trout inside and out with salt and pepper to taste. Slip 1 slice of ham inside each trout. Wrap a second ham slice around the center of each trout, leaving the head and tail exposed. Skewer the cavity closed with toothpicks or tie the fish around the middle with kitchen string.

In a large frying pan over medium heat, warm the olive oil. Place some flour in a strong plastic bag and, one at a time, add the trout and dust with flour, coating the fish evenly. Fry, turning once, until golden on both sides, about 4 minutes per side. Transfer to a warmed platter or individual plates.

Remove the toothpicks or string from the trout. Serve hot with lemon halves.

Serves 4

Mixed Meat Kabobs

12 oz (375 g) lean tender beef tenderloin (fillet) or rump

2 tablespoons light soy sauce

2 teaspoons sugar

1 tablespoon dry sherry or brandy

Salt and ground black pepper

6 baby lamb cutlets, bone trimmed

1 clove garlic, minced

3 sheeps' kidneys

3 slices (rashers) fat bacon

3 spicy sausages

1 large boneless, skinless chicken breast half

2 tablespoons olive or canola oil

Lemon pepper

6 small bay leaves

6 button mushrooms

6 large cherry tomatoes

2 tablespoons olive oil or melted butter

Cut the beef into 1-inch (2.5-cm) cubes. In a shallow bowl, combine the soy sauce, sugar, sherry or brandy, and salt and pepper to taste. Add the beef cubes, turn to coat the meat with the mixture, and leave to marinate at room temperature for 20 minutes.

Meanwhile, rub the lamb cutlets with garlic and set aside. Cut the kidneys in halves, remove the core, and wrap a half slice of bacon around each. Cut the sausages in halves and set aside. Cut the chicken crosswise into 6 pieces and rub with oil, then sprinkle with lemon pepper.

When the beef has been marinated, thread each type of meat in turn onto oiled metal skewers, adding a bay leaf, mushroom, and tomato to each. Brush with oil or melted butter and grill (barbecue) or broil (grill), turning frequently, until done to your liking. Serve immediately.

Serves 6

Chicken Curry with Three Accompaniments

1/4 cup (2 oz/60 g) ghee or canola oil

2 lb (1 kg) skinless, boneless chicken breasts, sliced

2 onions, chopped

3 cloves garlic, minced

2 teaspoons peeled and grated fresh ginger

1 tablespoon curry powder

1 teaspoon turmeric

2 teaspoons ground cumin

1 teaspoon garam masala

1/2 teaspoon chopped fresh chili

1 x 13-oz (410-g) can tomatoes

1 cup (8 fl oz/250 ml) chicken stock

2 cups (16 fl oz/500 ml) unsweetened coconut cream

1 green bell pepper (capsicum), chopped

8 oz (250 g) cauliflower, chopped

3 Asian (slender) eggplants (aubergines), chopped

1 tablespoon chopped cilantro (fresh coriander)

THREE ACCOMPANIMENTS

1/2 cup (4 fl oz/125 ml) plain yogurt

1 small green cucumber, finely chopped

1 tablespoon chopped fresh mint

2 small tomatoes, finely chopped

1 tablespoon fresh lime juice

1 tablespoon chopped cilantro (fresh coriander)

1/3 cup (2 1/2 oz/80 g) mango chutney

CHICKEN CURRY WITH THREE ACCOMPANIMENTS

In a large frying pan, heat 3 tablespoons of the ghee or oil over high heat. Add a few chicken slices and cook, stirring, over high heat until golden brown. Transfer the cooked chicken to a plate. Repeat in batches with the remaining chicken slices.

Preheat an oven to 450°F (220°C/Gas Mark 6).

Add to the pan the remaining ghee or oil, the onions, garlic, ginger, curry powder, turmeric, cumin, garam masala, and chili. Cook over medium heat, stirring, until the onion is soft and the spices fragrant, about 5 minutes. Add the tomatoes, stock, and coconut cream. Bring to a boil. Add the vegetables, reduce heat, and simmer, uncovered, until the vegetables are tender and the sauce is thick, about 20 minutes.

Return the chicken to the pan and simmer until the chicken is cooked through, about 10 minutes. Stir in the cilantro.

For the 3 accompaniments, combine the yogurt, cucumber, and mint in a small bowl and mix well. Combine the tomatoes, lime juice, and cilantro in another small bowl and mix well. Place the mango chutney in another small bowl.

Serve the chicken curry with the 3 accompaniments.

Serves 4

Grilled Tuna Kabobs

1/4 cup (2 fl oz/60 ml) olive oil

3 tablespoons fresh lemon juice

1/2 teaspoon paprika

1 1/2–2 lb (750 g–1 kg) fresh tuna steaks, cut into 1-inch (2.5-cm) cubes

24 small whole bay leaves

2 lemons, thinly sliced

2 green, red, or yellow bell peppers (capsicums), seeded and cut into 1-inch (2.5-cm) squares

16 firm ripe cherry tomatoes

Salt and ground black pepper

Lemon wedges, for garnish

In a small bowl, whisk the olive oil, lemon juice, and paprika until combined. Add the tuna cubes and stir to coat. Marinate at room temperature, stirring occasionally, for 30 minutes or in the refrigerator for 45 minutes.

Meanwhile, in a shallow dish, soak the bay leaves in warm water for 30 minutes. Drain and set aside.

Preheat a two-sided electric indoor grill (barbecue) or ridged grill pan according to the manufacturer's instructions.

Thread skewers with the tuna cubes, bay leaves, lemon, bell pepper, and tomatoes, leaving a little space between the pieces. Season with salt and pepper.

If you are using the two-sided grill, place the kabobs on the grill, close the cover, and cook, in batches as necessary, until the tuna is no longer pink in the center, 3–4 minutes.

If you are using the grill pan, cook the kabobs, in batches as necessary, until the tuna is no longer pink in the center, 5–6 minutes, turning once midway through cooking.

Serve the kabobs on a platter garnished with lemon wedges.

Serves 4

Chicken Cacciatore

3 tablespoons olive oil

1 onion, chopped

4 oz (125 g) bacon, chopped

3 cloves garlic, minced

4 chicken drumsticks

4 chicken thighs

2 × 14 oz (440 g) cans chopped tomatoes

½ cup (4 fl oz/125 ml) white wine

5 oz (160 g) white mushrooms

2 teaspoons dried oregano

½ tablespoon brown sugar

Salt and black pepper

Heat half the oil in a large saucepan, add the onion and bacon and cook, stirring, until they are soft and golden. Add the garlic and cook for 1 minute. Remove the onion mixture from the pan. Add

the remaining oil to the pan, along with the chicken drumsticks and thighs, and cook, turning, until the meat is browned. Return the onion mixture to the pan.

Add the tomatoes, wine, mushrooms, and oregano; bring to a boil. Reduce heat, cover, and simmer for 35 minutes or until the chicken is tender. During the last 10 minutes of cooking time, remove the saucepan lid and allow the liquid to reduce a little. Add the brown sugar, season with salt and black pepper, and serve immediately.

Serves 4

Stuffed Chicken Breasts with Bell Pepper Coulis

3 oz (100 g) cream cheese, at room temperature

2 tablespoons grated Parmesan cheese

1 tablespoon capers

1 tablespoon milk

1 clove garlic, minced

Pepper to taste

4 skinless, boneless chicken breast halves (1 lb/500 g total)

1 tablespoon olive oil or canola oil

1/4 cup (2 fl oz/60 ml) dry white wine

BELL PEPPER COULIS

2 red bell peppers (capsicums), roasted and peeled, or 1 x 6-oz (190-g) jar roasted bell peppers, drained

1 tablespoon olive oil or vegetable oil

2 cloves garlic, minced

1/4 cup (2 fl oz/60 ml) half-and-half (half cream) or light (single) cream

2 teaspoons anchovy paste

1 tablespoon capers

2 bundles thin asparagus, lightly steamed

Preheat an oven to 350°F (180°C/Gas Mark 4).

For the chicken breasts, in a small mixing bowl, combine the cream cheese, Parmesan cheese, capers, milk, garlic, and pepper. Set aside.

Place each breast half between 2 pieces of plastic wrap. Working from the center to the edges, pound the chicken with the flat side of a meat mallet to 1/8 inch (3 mm) thick. Remove the plastic wrap. Spread one-fourth of the cream cheese mixture over each breast half. Fold in the sides and roll up, jelly-roll (Swiss-roll) style, pressing the edges to seal.

In a large frying pan over medium-high heat, warm the oil. Add the chicken and brown on both sides, about 5 minutes total. Transfer chicken to an 8-cup (2-qt/2-l) baking dish. Pour the wine over the chicken and bake, uncovered, until cooked through, 20–25 minutes.

For the coulis, in a blender or food processor, blend or process the bell peppers until smooth. Set aside. In a small saucepan over medium heat, warm the remaining oil. Add the garlic and cook, stirring, until tender but not brown, about 2 minutes. Add the puréed bell peppers, half-and-half or cream, anchovy paste, and capers. Heat through.

Divide the coulis between 4 warmed plates and top each with a chicken breast and some asparagus. Serve hot.

Serves 4

Sea Perch with Herb Butter

2 lemons

4 sea perch fillets

HERB BUTTER

¼ cup (2 oz/60 g) butter

½ teaspoon salt

⅓ teaspoon black pepper

2 teaspoons minced parsley

1 teaspoon chopped dill

1 teaspoon chopped chives

1 tablespoon minced red bell pepper (capsicum)

1 clove garlic, minced

4 small zucchini (courgettes)

Dill sprigs, to serve

Cut 1 lemon in half and squeeze 1 half over the fish. Cut the remaining half into 2 wedges and the other lemon into 4 wedges and set aside.

For the herb butter, mash the butter with the salt, pepper, herbs, bell pepper, and garlic. Spread over the fish. Place the fish in a frying pan and fry until cooked through, turning once.

Slice the zucchini lengthwise, without cutting through the stalk end. Drop into boiling, lightly salted water and simmer until just tender. Drain well. Arrange 1 zucchini

in a fan shape on each of 4 warmed serving plates. Place 1 fish fillet on each plate, along with some of the lemon wedges and dill sprigs. Spoon any sauce left in the pan over the fish. Serve immediately.

Serves 4

Ginger Chicken with Mushrooms

1 cup (6 oz/190 g) small snow peas (mangetouts), tips and strings removed

1/2 cup (2 1/2 oz/80 g) loose-pack frozen peas

3/4 cup (6 fl oz/190 ml) half-and-half (half cream) or light (single) cream

2 teaspoons cornstarch (cornflour)

Salt and pepper to taste

1 tablespoon canola oil

2 teaspoons peeled and grated fresh ginger

2 1/2 cups (8 oz/250 g) fresh shiitake mushrooms or other mushrooms, stems removed, caps sliced

12 oz (375 g) chicken breast meat, cut into thin bite-size strips

1/4 cup (1/4 oz/10 g) chopped fresh flat-leaf (Italian) parsley

In a pan over medium heat, boil all the peas until the snow peas are crisp-tender, about 1 minute. Drain and set aside.

In a bowl, stir together the half-and-half, cornstarch, and salt and pepper. Set aside.

In a wok or large frying pan, over medium-high heat, warm the oil. (Add more oil if necessary during cooking.) Stir-fry the ginger for 30 seconds.

Add the mushrooms and stir-fry until tender, about 2 minutes. Remove vegetables from the wok.

Add the chicken strips to the hot wok. Stir-fry until cooked through, 3–4 minutes. Push the chicken to the edges of wok. Stir the half-and-half mixture and pour into the center of the wok. Cook, stirring, until the mixture is thick and bubbly. Return vegetables to the wok.

Stir all the ingredients together to coat with the sauce. Cook, stirring, until heated through, 1 minute. Sprinkle with the parsley and serve immediately.

Serves 4

187

Mexican Marinated Chicken

½ cup (4 fl oz/125 ml) fresh orange juice

2 tablespoons fresh lime juice

1 dried chipotle chili, stems removed and seeded

1 cup (8 oz/250 g) tomato and chili salsa

¼ cup (2 fl oz/60 ml) olive oil

1 teaspoon salt

4 skinless, boneless chicken breast halves (1 lb/500 g total)

Fresh orange slices (optional)

Cilantro (fresh coriander) sprigs (optional)

In a small saucepan over high heat, combine the orange juice, lime juice, and chili. Bring to a boil. Reduce the heat to low and simmer, uncovered, until the chili is plump, about 5 minutes. Remove the pan from the heat and allow to cool.

In the bowl of a food processor, combine the cooled mixture, the salsa, oil, and the salt. Process to a purée.

Place the chicken breasts in a shallow nonaluminum dish. Pour the purée evenly over the chicken. Cover and marinate in the refrigerator for 2–4 hours.

Preheat a broiler (griller) or heat a grill (barbecue) to hot.

Remove the chicken breasts from the marinade. Discard marinade. Place the chicken breasts on the cooking rack, skin side down if broiling and skin side up if grilling. Broil, 4 inches (10 cm) from heat, or grill, 2–3 minutes each side. Continue to cook, turning every 2–3 minutes to avoid burning, until cooked through, 12–20 minutes.

Transfer the chicken to a warmed platter. Garnish with orange slices and cilantro sprigs, if desired. Serve immediately.

Serves 4

Italian Chicken with Pesto Mayonnaise

2 red bell peppers (capsicums), quartered

1 bunch (1¼ lb/600 g) leaf (English) spinach, washed

6 skinless, boneless chicken breast halves (about 1½ lb/750 g)

5 oz (160 g) thinly sliced mild salami

¼ cup (1 oz/30 g) drained, oil-packed, sun-dried tomatoes, thinly sliced

5 oz (160 g) shredded mozzarella cheese

Black pepper to taste

1 tablespoon olive oil

1 clove garlic, minced

PESTO MAYONNAISE

1 cup (1 oz/30 g) lightly packed basil leaves

1 clove garlic, minced

2 tablespoons grated Parmesan cheese

¼ cup (2 fl oz/60 ml) olive oil

½ cup (4 fl oz/125 ml) bought mayonnaise

Salt and pepper to taste

Preheat an oven to 375°F (190°C/Gas Mark 4). Preheat a broiler (griller).

Broil (grill) bell peppers, skin side up, 4–5 inches (10–12 cm) from the heat, until the skin blisters and blackens, about 10 minutes. Place bell peppers in a plastic bag, seal, and leave for 10 minutes or until cool enough to handle. (The steam created will make the bell peppers easier to peel.) Peel and cut into strips.

Boil, steam, or microwave the spinach until wilted. Drain well and pat dry with paper towels.

Place each chicken breast half between plastic wrap and, using the flat side of a meat mallet, gently pound to even out the thickness and square off. Lay the spinach leaves evenly over the chicken, then top with salami, roasted peppers, tomatoes, and mozzarella cheese. Sprinkle with pepper and press down firmly. Roll up tightly and secure each roll with string at 1-inch (2.5-cm) intervals. Mix together the oil and garlic and brush over the rolls. Bake until cooked through, about 1 hour. Let cool, then refrigerate for several hours.

For the pesto mayonnaise, in a blender or food processor, blend or process basil, garlic, Parmesan cheese, and oil until smooth. In a bowl, combine basil mixture, mayonnaise, and salt and pepper. Mix well. Keep tightly covered until required.

Remove the string from the chicken and slice thinly. Serve with the pesto mayonnaise.

Serves 4 to 6

Middle Eastern Lamb Skewers

SAUCE

2 cups (16 fl oz/500 ml) plain (natural) yogurt

1 clove garlic, minced

2 tablespoons olive oil

1 1/2 teaspoons red wine vinegar or fresh lemon juice

1 tablespoon chopped fresh parsley

1 tablespoon chopped fresh mint

Salt and ground black pepper

MEATBALLS

1 lb (500 g) ground (minced) lamb

1 large egg, lightly beaten

1 small yellow onion, grated

1 clove garlic, minced

1 1/2 teaspoons chopped fresh thyme

1/2 teaspoon salt

1/4 teaspoon ground black pepper

Green salad leaves

8 slices tomato

4 slices red onion

To make the sauce, line a strainer with cheesecloth or several moistened paper coffee filters. Set the strainer over a bowl, add the yogurt, cover and refrigerate for 4–6 hours or until the yogurt has drained, thickened, and reduced to about 1 cup (8 fl oz/250 ml).

Discard the drained liquid. In a small bowl stir together the thickened yogurt with the garlic, olive oil, vinegar or lemon juice, parsley, and mint. Season the yogurt mixture with salt and pepper. Cover and refrigerate.

To make the meatballs, in a bowl combine the lamb, egg, onion, garlic, thyme, salt, and pepper and mix with your hands until well combined. Shape the meat mixture into sixteen 1 1/2-inch (4-cm) balls.

Preheat a two-sided electric indoor grill (barbecue) or ridged grill pan according to the manufacturer's instructions.

If you are using the two-sided grill, place the meatballs on the grill, close the cover, and cook until they are no longer pink in the center, about 3 minutes.

If you are using the grill pan, cook until the meatballs are no longer pink in the center, about 5 minutes, turning them several times during cooking to brown them on all sides.

Serve the meatballs on the salad leaves with the sliced tomato and onion, and the yogurt sauce.

Serves 4

Fish Fillets with Red Bell Pepper, Coriander and Lemon Sauce

RED BELL PEPPER SAUCE

2 teaspoons coriander seeds

2 tablespoons fresh lemon juice

2 tablespoons water

1/4 cup (1 1/2 oz/45 g) roasted, peeled, and chopped red bell pepper (capsicum)

1/3 cup (2 1/2 fl oz/80 ml) olive oil

1 teaspoon salt, plus extra to taste

1/2 teaspoon ground white pepper, plus extra to taste

4 fillets of firm white fish, such as monkfish, sea bass, or cod, 4 oz (125 g) each, trimmed

2 tablespoons chopped fresh parsley

For the sauce, a blender, combine the coriander seeds, lemon juice, water, bell pepper, olive oil, the 1 teaspoon salt, and 1/2 teaspoon white pepper. Blend at high speed until smooth and creamy, about 1 minute. Pour purée through a fine-mesh sieve into a clean bowl. Set aside.

Sprinkle both sides of each fish fillet with salt and pepper to taste. Place on a steamer rack over (not touching) gently boiling water. Cover and steam until just cooked through, 6–7 minutes.

Transfer fillets to warmed individual plates. Spoon the sauce evenly over the top and sides of the fish. Sprinkle with the parsley and serve at once.

Serves 6 to 8 as an appetizer or 4 as a main course

Shrimp Skewers with Mango Salsa

SHRIMP

¼ cup (2 fl oz/60 ml) olive oil

3 cloves garlic, thinly sliced

3 tablespoons fresh lime juice

½ teaspoon salt

¼ teaspoon ground black pepper

1–1½ lb (500–750 g) large shrimp (prawns), peeled and deveined

MANGO SALSA

1 large ripe mango, peeled and diced

4 green (spring) onions, white and green parts, trimmed and thinly sliced

1 English (hothouse) cucumber, seeded and diced

1 small jalapeño chili, seeded and very finely diced

2–3 tablespoons chopped cilantro (fresh coriander)

2 tablespoons fresh lime juice

Lime wedges, for garnish

To prepare the shrimp, in a small saucepan heat the olive oil and garlic over low heat until fragrant, about 3 minutes. Transfer to a medium bowl.

Add the lime juice, salt, and pepper; stir to combine. Cool slightly. Add the shrimp and stir to coat them evenly. Marinate the shrimp at room temperature for 30 minutes, stirring occasionally.

Meanwhile, for the mango salsa, in a medium bowl, stir together all the salsa ingredients. Season with salt to taste and set aside.

Preheat a large two-sided electric indoor grill (barbecue) or ridged grill pan according to the manufacturer's instructions.

Thread the shrimp onto skewers, passing the skewer through points near both the head and tail sections of each shrimp, leaving a little space between the pieces.

If you are using the two-sided grill, place the skewers on the grill, close the cover, and cook, in batches as necessary, until the shrimp turn pink and are opaque throughout, 2–3 minutes.

If you are using the grill pan, cook the shrimp, in batches as necessary, until they turn pink and are opaque throughout, 4–6 minutes, turning them once midway through cooking.

Serve the skewers with lime wedges and the salsa.

Serves 4

Spicy Yogurt Chicken

MARINADE

1 cup (8 fl oz/250 ml) plain low-fat yogurt

2 tablespoons chopped cilantro (fresh coriander) or fresh parsley, plus extra for garnish

1 tablespoon curry powder

2 cloves garlic, minced

1 teaspoon ground ginger

1 teaspoon paprika

2–3 teaspoons fresh lime juice or fresh lemon juice

Salt to taste

4 skinless chicken legs (about 2 lb/1 kg total)

2 tablespoons (1 oz/30 g) margarine

For the marinade, in a small mixing bowl, stir together the yogurt, the 2 tablespoons cilantro or parsley, the curry powder, garlic, ginger, paprika, lime or lemon juice, and salt.

Place the chicken legs in a large, strong plastic bag set into a shallow dish. Pour the marinade into the plastic bag. Seal the bag and turn it to coat the chicken completely with marinade. Marinate the chicken in the refrigerator for 2–24 hours, turning the bag occasionally.

In a large frying pan over medium heat, melt the margarine. Add the chicken legs and the marinade and bring to a boil. Reduce the heat to low, cover, and simmer until the chicken is cooked through, 45–50 minutes.

Transfer the chicken to a serving platter. Bring the marinade to a boil and gently boil until slightly thickened, about 5 minutes. Pour over the chicken and garnish with the extra cilantro or parsley. Serve immediately.

Serves 4

Microwave Chicken Paprika

1 tablespoon (1/2 oz/15 g) butter

1 tablespoon olive oil

1 large onion, chopped

1 clove garlic, minced

2 teaspoons paprika, or to taste

1 cup (8 fl oz/250 ml) hot chicken stock

4 lb (2 kg) skinless chicken pieces

1 teaspoon all-purpose (plain) flour

1/2 cup (4 fl oz/125 ml) sour cream

In a medium microwave-safe casserole, combine the butter, oil, onion, garlic, and paprika. Mix well. Cook on high (100%) until onion is transparent and begins to color slightly, about 1 minute. Add the stock and chicken. Mix well. Cook on high for 6–8 minutes, rearranging the chicken after 4 minutes. Reduce to medium-high (70%) and cook until the chicken is cooked through, 10 minutes, rearranging the chicken after 5 minutes.

In a small bowl, mix together the flour and sour cream. Slowly stir into the casserole dish, mixing well. Cook on medium-high for 1–2 minutes more.

Serve the chicken with a green salad, if desired.

Serves 6 to 8

Chicken Provençal

2 cups (8 oz/250 g) cubed peeled eggplant (aubergine)

2 tomatoes, peeled, seeded, and chopped

1 onion, halved and thinly sliced

1 red bell pepper (capsicum), cut into thin strips

1 green bell pepper (capsicum), cut into thin strips

1/4 cup (2 fl oz/60 ml) red or dry white wine or chicken stock

2 tablespoons chopped fresh basil or 1 1/2 teaspoons dried basil

2 cloves garlic, minced

1/2 teaspoon salt

4 boneless, skinless chicken breast halves (about 1 lb/500 g total)

Salt

1 tablespoon olive oil or vegetable oil

1/2 teaspoon paprika

In a large saucepan, combine the eggplant, tomato, onion, red and green bell pepper, wine or chicken stock, basil, garlic, and salt. Bring to a boil over medium-high heat, then reduce the heat and simmer, covered, for 10 minutes. Uncover and simmer for about 5 minutes more, or until the vegetables are tender and nearly all of the liquid has evaporated.

Meanwhile, rinse the chicken; pat dry. Place each breast half between 2 pieces of plastic wrap. Working from the center to the edges, pound the chicken lightly, with the flat side of a meat mallet, to a 1/2-inch (1-cm) thickness. Remove the plastic wrap. Sprinkle the chicken lightly with salt. In a large frying pan, warm the oil and paprika over medium-high heat. Add the chicken and cook until tender and no pink remains, 4–6 minutes, turning once.

To serve, spoon the vegetable mixture onto warmed serving plates and top with the chicken.

Serves 4

Roast Leg of Lamb with Yogurt

1 leg of lamb on the bone,
5–6 lb (2.5–3 kg)

6 cloves garlic, plus 2 teaspoons
chopped garlic

2 teaspoons plus 3 tablespoons
chopped fresh rosemary

1/3 cup (2 1/2 fl oz/80 ml) olive oil

1/4 cup (2 fl oz/60 ml) fresh
lemon juice

Salt and ground pepper

1 1/2 cups (12 fl oz/375 ml)
whole-milk or low-fat plain yogurt

1 teaspoon ground cinnamon

1/2 teaspoon all-purpose (plain)
flour

Using a small, sharp knife, cut about 12 slits, each about 1/2 inch (1 cm) deep, in the leg of lamb, spacing them evenly. Cut 3 of the garlic cloves into thin slivers and place in a small bowl with the 2 teaspoons of rosemary. Mix well and insert the garlic mixture in the slits.

Finely chop the remaining 3 garlic cloves and place in a small bowl. Add 2 tablespoons of the rosemary, 2 tablespoons of the olive oil, and 2 tablespoons of the lemon juice and mix well. Rub this mixture all over the leg of lamb. Cover and let marinate for 2 hours at room temperature or overnight in the refrigerator.

Preheat an oven to 350°F (180°C/Gas Mark 4).

Place the lamb in a roasting pan and sprinkle with salt and pepper to taste.

Whisk the remaining olive oil with the remaining lemon juice in a small bowl. Add the remaining rosemary and the 2 teaspoons chopped garlic. Roast the lamb, basting every 20 minutes with the oil-lemon mixture, for 1 1/4 hours.

Whisk the yogurt with the cinnamon and flour in another bowl. Spoon the mixture over the lamb and continue to roast for about 15 minutes longer for medium-rare, or until the lamb is done to your liking and the yogurt sauce forms a crust. To test, insert an instant-read thermometer into the thickest part of the leg away from the bone; it should register 125°F (52°C) for medium-rare. Transfer the lamb to a warmed serving platter and leave to rest in a warm place for 8–10 minutes before carving. Serve hot.

Serves 6

About Rosemary

Rosemary is one of the highlights of the herb or kitchen garden. Native to the Mediterranean, it has a popular place in Italian, French, and Greek cuisines. Its sweet, strong flavor goes particularly well with lamb, as well as with vegetables.

Rosemary's name comes from the Latin *rosmarinus*, meaning "sea dew," and it loves to grow by the sea. Later it was called Rose of Mary, or rosemary, in honor of the Virgin Mary.

The scent of rosemary stays on the fingers a long time after it has been touched; this may be the reason that it is widely known as the symbol of remembrance. Europeans carried rosemary (and sometimes still do) at weddings and funerals because they believed it would aid their memories of promises and people.

Rosemary oil is used in perfumes. Rosemary is also known for its pest-repellent and medicinal properties: The dried leaves have been used in sachets to repel moths, and to brew tea for stomach aches and headaches.

Grilled Lemongrass Beef

1 lb (500 g) beef chuck, rump, or sirloin, in 1 piece

LEMONGRASS MARINADE

1 tablespoon toasted sesame seeds

2 lemongrass stalks, tender heart section only, finely chopped

3 Asian (purple) shallots, minced

3 cloves garlic

1 small red chili, seeded

1/2 tablespoon sugar

1 1/2 tablespoons fish sauce

1 tablespoon fresh lemon juice

1/4 teaspoon ground black pepper

1 1/2 teaspoons toasted (Asian) sesame oil

1 tablespoon peanut or canola oil

LIME DIPPING SAUCE

1 clove garlic, minced

1 small fresh red chili, seeded and minced

1 1/2 tablespoons sugar

1/4 cup (2 fl oz/60 ml) fresh lime juice, including pulp

1/4 cup (2 fl oz/60 ml) Thai or Vietnamese fish sauce

1/2 cup (4 fl oz/125 ml) water

Wrap the beef in plastic wrap and place in the freezer until partially frozen, about 1 hour.

For the marinade, in a blender or mini food processor, combine the sesame seeds, lemongrass,

shallots, garlic, chili, and sugar. Process to a smooth paste. Transfer to a large bowl and add the fish sauce, lemon juice, pepper, sesame oil, and peanut or vegetable oil.

For the lime dipping sauce, in a mortar, combine the garlic, chili, and sugar. Mash with a pestle to form a paste. Add the lime juice and pulp, fish sauce, and water and stir until the sugar is dissolved. Strain the sauce into a bowl and use immediately, or cover tightly and refrigerate for up to 5 days.

Slice the beef very thinly across the grain. Add to the marinade, toss to coat, and leave for at least

1 hour at room temperature, or cover and refrigerate for up to 4 hours.

Preheat a ridged grill pan over medium-high heat until hot, then spread the beef slices over it. (Or, prepare a fire in a charcoal grill/barbecue. When the coals are ash white, lay the beef slices flat on the grill rack about 4 inches/10 cm above the coals.) Cook, turning once, until the beef is cooked through, about 30 seconds on each side.

Transfer the beef slices to warmed serving plates and serve with the dipping sauce.

Serves 6

Grilled Five-Spice Chicken

FIVE-SPICE MARINADE

2 teaspoons fresh ginger, peeled and grated

4 cloves garlic, chopped

2 purple (Asian) shallots, chopped

1 tablespoon brown sugar

1/2 teaspoon salt

1/4 teaspoon ground black pepper

1/2 teaspoon five-spice powder

2 tablespoons Vietnamese or Thai fish sauce

2 tablespoons soy sauce

1 tablespoon dry sherry

4 large skinless, boneless chicken breast halves (about 1 lb/500 g)

Lime Dipping Sauce (page 204)

For the marinade, combine the ginger, garlic, shallots, brown sugar, and salt in a mortar or mini food processor. Mash with a pestle or process to a smooth paste. Transfer to a large, shallow bowl. Add the pepper, five-spice powder, fish sauce, soy sauce, and sherry and stir well. Add the chicken breasts and turn to coat them thoroughly with the marinade. Cover and marinate in the refrigerator for a few hours or as long as overnight.

Preheat a grill (barbecue) or broiler (griller) and cook the chicken over medium heat until just cooked through, turning once. Test by pressing the thickest part; it should feel firm.

Serve the chicken hot with the lime dipping sauce.

Serves 4

Neapolitan Braised Beef Braciole

1 lb (500 g) top beef round, cut into 4 thin slices

4 thin slices (about 4 oz/125 g) smoked baked ham

4 thin slices (about 4 oz/125 g) Provolone cheese

2 tablespoons chopped fresh parsley

4 teaspoons chopped garlic

1 small carrot, peeled and chopped

4 teaspoons chopped celery, plus 2 tablespoons extra

3 tablespoons extra virgin olive oil

1/4 cup (1 1/2 oz/45 g) chopped red (Spanish) onion

1/2 cup (4 fl oz/125 ml) Chianti or other Italian red wine, plus 2 tablespoons extra

2 x 28-oz (880-g) cans plum (Roma) tomatoes, drained and puréed

Salt and ground pepper

Place each beef slice between 2 sheets of plastic wrap and, using the flat side of a meat mallet, pound until about 1/8 inch (3 mm) thick. Place 1 ham slice on top of each beef slice, and top with a cheese slice.

In a bowl, combine the parsley, half the garlic, 1 tablespoon of the carrot, and the 4 teaspoons celery. Sprinkle the mixture evenly over the center of each cheese slice. Beginning at 1 end of each beef slice, roll up tightly and secure the seam with toothpicks. Seal the ends with toothpicks as well, to keep the filling from spilling out.

Heat the oil in a deep saucepan over medium heat, and cook the beef rolls for 4–5 minutes, or until browned well on all sides. Reduce the heat to medium-low, add the remaining carrot, 2 tablespoons celery, and the onion and cook for 2 minutes. Add the remaining 2 teaspoons garlic and cook for 1–2 minutes, or until fragrant.

Increase the heat to high, add the ½ cup (4 fl oz/125 ml) red wine, and deglaze the pan by stirring to dislodge the browned bits from the bottom of the pan. Boil for 1 minute, then add the puréed tomatoes. Return to a boil, then reduce the heat to low and simmer, uncovered, for about 1½ hours, or until the beef rolls are tender when pierced with a fork.

Add the remaining 2 tablespoons red wine and continue to simmer for 2 minutes longer. Season to taste with salt and pepper. Spoon onto warmed individual plates, remove the toothpicks, and serve immediately.

Serves 4

Stir-Fried Chicken and Asparagus

1 egg white, lightly beaten

1 tablespoon cornstarch (cornflour)

1 tablespoon dry white wine

1 clove garlic, minced

Salt and pepper to taste

1 lb (500 g) chicken thigh meat, cut into thin, bite-size strips

2 tablespoons chili sauce

2 tablespoons soy sauce

1 tablespoon wine vinegar

1–1½ teaspoons chili oil

1 tablespoon vegetable oil

1 lb (500 g) fresh asparagus spears, diagonally sliced into 2-inch (5-cm) pieces

1 red bell pepper (capsicum), cut into bite-size strips

4 green (spring) onions, diagonally sliced into 1-inch (2.5-cm) pieces

In a medium mixing bowl, stir together the egg white, cornstarch, wine, garlic, and salt and pepper. Stir in the chicken strips. Cover and let stand at room temperature for 20–30 minutes. Do not drain.

Meanwhile, in a small mixing bowl, stir together the chili sauce, soy sauce, wine vinegar, and chili oil. Set aside.

In a wok or large frying pan over medium heat, warm the vegetable oil. Add half of each of the asparagus, bell pepper, and green onions and stir-fry until crisp-tender, 3–4 minutes. Remove from the wok. Repeat with the remaining vegetables.

Add the undrained chicken strips to the hot wok. Stir-fry until cooked through, 3–4 minutes. Return the cooked vegetables to the wok. Stir the chili sauce mixture and mix into the chicken and vegetables. Cover and cook until heated through, about 1 minute. Divide among warmed bowls and serve.

Serves 4

Swordfish with Spinach and Citrus Vinaigrette

¼ cup (2 fl oz/60 ml) water

2 tablespoons (1 oz/30 g) unsalted butter

⅓ cup (2½ fl oz/80 ml) olive oil

1¼ lb (600 g) spinach leaves, stems removed, leaves thoroughly washed

Salt and ground black pepper

4 swordfish steaks, about 5 oz (160 g) each

Juice of ½ orange

Juice of ½ lemon

Juice of ¼ grapefruit

¼ cup (2 fl oz/60 ml) veal stock or chicken stock

In a large saucepan over high heat, combine the water, butter, and 2 tablespoons of the olive oil. Once the butter has melted completely, add the spinach leaves and salt and pepper to taste. Cover and cook, stirring every 20–30 seconds, until the spinach is wilted, about 2 minutes. Remove from the heat, cover, and set aside.

In a large frying pan over high heat, warm 1 tablespoon of the olive oil. Sprinkle both sides of the swordfish steaks with salt and pepper to taste. Place the swordfish steaks in the hot pan and cook, turning once, until done to your liking, 1–2 minutes on each side for medium-rare. Transfer the fish steaks to a plate and cover to keep warm.

Pour off any oil remaining in the sauté pan and place over high heat. When the pan is hot, pour in the citrus juices and deglaze the pan by stirring to dislodge any browned bits from the bottom of the pan. Boil until the liquid is reduced by half, then add the veal or chicken stock and salt and pepper to taste. Return to a boil and stir in the remaining 2 tablespoons olive oil. Remove from the heat.

Drain the spinach in a sieve and divide equally among warmed individual plates. Place the swordfish steaks on top of the spinach and spoon the citrus mixture evenly over the steaks. Serve immediately.

Serves 4

Prosciutto-Wrapped Shrimp Skewers

MARINADE

2 tablespoons fruity Italian white wine

2 tablespoons olive oil

1 tablespoon fresh lemon juice

8 x 2-inch (5-cm) strips lemon zest

3 large cloves garlic, minced

1 teaspoon fresh thyme leaves or 1/2 teaspoon dried

1/2 teaspoon crumbled bay leaf

Ground black pepper

SKEWERS

16 jumbo shrimp (prawns) (about 1 lb/500 g), peeled and deveined

2 medium zucchini (courgettes), trimmed and cut lengthwise into 1/8-inch (3-mm) thick slices

8 slices prosciutto, cut paper thin, trimmed of excess fat, and cut in half lengthwise

For the marinade, in a shallow, nonreactive dish, combine all of the marinade ingredients and mix well to combine. Add the shrimp and turn to coat. Cover the dish and refrigerate for 30 minutes to 2 hours.

Preheat a two-sided electric indoor grill (barbecue) or ridged grill pan according to the manufacturer's instructions.

If you are using the two-sided grill, arrange the zucchini slices on the grill, close the cover, and cook the zucchini slices until just soft and pliable, about 3 minutes. Let cool slightly.

To prepare the skewers, remove the shrimp from the marinade, reserving the lemon strips. Wrap 1 slice of prosciutto around a shrimp, then wrap it with a zucchini slice. Thread the shrimp onto a skewer. Repeat with the remaining shrimp, prosciutto, and zucchini, placing 4 shrimp on each skewer, leaving a little space between the pieces. Thread 2 of the reserved lemon strips on each skewer.

Place the skewers on the grill, close the cover, and cook until the shrimp is just cooked through, about 3 minutes.

If you are using the grill pan, cook the zucchini slices, in batches as necessary, until they are just soft and pliable, about 5 minutes, turning once midway through cooking time. Let them cool slightly.

Prepare the skewers as described above. Cook until the shrimp is just cooked through,

about 6 minutes, turning once midway through cooking.

Arrange the skewers on a platter, garnish with thyme sprigs, and serve immediately.

Serves 4

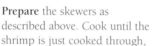

Fish Grilled in Grape Leaves

MARINADE

1/4 cup (2 fl oz/60 ml) olive oil

2 tablespoons chopped fresh parsley or fennel fronds

2 teaspoons chopped fresh thyme or oregano

Juice of 1 small lemon

1/2 teaspoon salt

1/4 teaspoon ground black pepper

FISH

2 lb (980 g) fresh large sardines, cleaned with heads left on, or 4 white fish fillets, such as cod, sea bass or hake, about 6 oz (180 g) each

Bottled grape leaves, rinsed and stems removed

Lemon wedges for garnish

For the marinade, in a shallow, nonreactive dish, whisk together the olive oil, parsley or fennel, thyme or oregano, lemon juice, salt, and pepper. Add the fish, turning to coat. Cover and refrigerate for 1–2 hours.

Preheat a two-sided electric indoor grill (barbecue) or ridged grill pan according to the manufacturer's instructions.

Remove the fish from the marinade, shaking off the excess. Wrap each fillet in 1 or 2 grape leaves, leaving the ends exposed.

If you are using the two-sided grill, place the fillets on the grill, close the cover, and cook until they are just opaque in the center, about 4 minutes. (Cook for 2–3 minutes per 1/2 inch/ 1 cm of thickness.)

If you are using the grill pan, cook the fillets until they are just opaque in the center, about 7 minutes, turning them once midway through cooking time. (Cook for 4–6 minutes per 1/2 inch/1 cm of thickness.)

Serve the fish with lemon wedges and any juices poured over the top.

Serves 4

Pork Ragout with Red Bell Peppers

3 tablespoons cumin seeds

2 tablespoons chopped garlic

1 teaspoon coarse (kosher) salt or sea salt

1 teaspoon ground pepper

1 tablespoon paprika

2 lb (1 kg) boneless pork shoulder

1/4 cup (2 fl oz/60 ml) olive oil

4 red bell peppers (capsicums), seeds and ribs removed, cut lengthwise into strips 1/2 inch (1 cm) wide

1 cup (8 fl oz/250 ml) dry white wine

1/2 cup (4 fl oz/125 ml) chicken stock

6 paper-thin lemon slices, cut into half rounds

1/2 cup (3/4 oz/20 g) chopped cilantro (fresh coriander)

Toast the cumin seeds in a small, dry frying pan over medium heat, swirling the pan occasionally, for 2–3 minutes, or until fragrant. Transfer to a spice grinder or peppermill and grind finely. Combine the ground cumin, garlic, salt, pepper, and paprika and mash in a mortar with a pestle to form a paste.

Cut the pork into 1-inch (2.5-cm) cubes. Place in a nonreactive bowl and rub the paste evenly over the

meat. Cover and marinate overnight in the refrigerator.

Bring the meat to room temperature. Heat the oil in a large frying pan over high heat and, working in batches, cook the pork for 5–8 minutes, or until browned on all sides. Using tongs or a slotted spoon, transfer the pork to a large, heavy pan. Add the bell pepper strips to the fat remaining in the pan and cook for 5 minutes, or until softened.

Transfer bell pepper strips to the pan containing the pork. Return the pan to high heat, add the wine, and deglaze the pan by stirring to dislodge any browned bits from the bottom of the pan. Add the pan juices to the pork and bell peppers. Add the stock and lemon slices and bring to a boil. Quickly reduce heat to low, cover, and simmer for 25 minutes, or until pork is very tender.

Stir in the cilantro, then taste and adjust the seasoning, if necessary. Spoon into a warmed serving dish and serve hot.

Serves 4 to 6

About Ginger

Native to the jungles of southern Asia, and now widely cultivated in warm climates around the world, ginger has been valued for centuries. It has been used in China as a flavoring and medicament for thousands of years, and was coming into Europe via the trade routes long before Roman times. A versatile ingredient with a warm, spicy flavor, it is used in ginger beer, baked goods, ice cream, preserves, and many savory dishes, and is indispensable in many Asian cuisines.

Often erroneously called a root, ginger is in fact a rhizome, or underground stem. Fresh ginger may be grated, chopped, crushed, or sliced for use in savory dishes such as curries and stir-fries. As is the case with garlic, ginger will have a stronger flavor when grated or crushed than when simply chopped or sliced. Ginger is also available dried and powdered, crystallized, preserved in syrup, and pickled.

Young ginger, which is the cream- and pink-colored shoots of the rhizome, has the most delicate flavor and texture. As ginger ages, it darkens and develops in flavor but also becomes more fibrous. Choose ginger that is hard and heavy, with a smooth, pale, shiny, unbroken skin. Reject rhizomes that are wrinkled or that feel soft or rubbery. Store fresh ginger in a cool, dry place for up to 3 days or in the refrigerator for up to 3 weeks. If refrigerating, first wrap it in a paper towel then place in a plastic bag; this prevents the development of mold. Store dried, powdered ginger in an airtight container in a cool, dark place for up to 6 months.

Stir-Fried Shrimp with Vegetables

12 large uncooked shrimp (prawns)

1 medium onion

2 green (spring) onions

3 tablespoons canola oil or vegetable oil

1 red bell pepper (capsicum), thinly sliced lengthwise

1 medium carrot, thinly sliced

3 thin slices fresh ginger, cut into fine shreds

12 snowpeas (mangetouts)

1/2 cup (4 fl oz/125 ml) light chicken stock or water

1 tablespoon light or low-sodium soy sauce

1 teaspoon cornstarch (cornflour)

Salt and ground white pepper

Chinese greens, steamed, to serve

Peel and devein the shrimp, leaving the last section of the shell and the tail intact. Cutting from top to base, slice the onion into narrow strips and separate the pieces. Cut the green onions into 1 3/4-inch (4.5-cm) lengths, then slice them lengthwise into fine shreds.

In a wok or large frying pan, warm the oil. Add the onion, bell pepper, and carrot and stir-fry until they begin to soften, 3–4 minutes; transfer to a plate. Stir-fry the shrimp until they change color and are barely cooked through, 2–3 minutes; remove from pan. Add the green onions, ginger, and snowpeas; stir-fry for 30 seconds. Return shrimp and vegetables to the pan.

Combine the stock, soy sauce, and cornstarch; add this mixture to the pan and stir over high heat until the sauce thickens. Season with salt and pepper. Serve over Chinese greens.

Serves 4

Hearty Chicken Casserole

2 tablespoons canola oil

4 lb (2 kg) chicken pieces

2 onions, sliced lengthwise

2 cloves garlic, minced

8 oz (250 g) thinly sliced speck or prosciutto

3 carrots, thickly sliced

2 stalks celery, thickly sliced

14 oz (440 g) canned crushed tomatoes

1/3 cup (2 1/2 fl oz/80 ml) tomato paste

1 cup (8 fl oz/250 ml) chicken stock

1 x 1-lb (500-g) can cannellini beans, rinsed and drained

1/3 cup (1/3 oz/10 g) chopped fresh basil

2 tablespoons chopped fresh oregano

In a large frying pan over high heat, warm the oil. Add some of the chicken pieces and fry, turning to brown evenly, about 5 minutes total. Do not cook through. Transfer to a plate. Repeat in batches with the remaining chicken.

Reduce heat to medium and add the onions, garlic, speck or prosciutto, carrots, and celery. Cook, stirring, until the onions are soft, about 5 minutes. Add the tomatoes, tomato paste, and stock. Bring to a boil, return the chicken to the pan, reduce the heat and simmer, uncovered, until the chicken is cooked through, about 15 minutes. Add the beans and herbs and simmer for 2–3 minutes. Divide among warmed bowls and serve.

Serves 6

Beef Kabobs with Minted Coconut Chutney

1 lb (500 g) lean tender beef (tenderloin/fillet or rump), cut into 1-inch (2.5-cm) cubes

1 small onion, grated

1–2 cloves garlic, minced

1 teaspoon grated fresh ginger

2 tablespoons canola oil, plus extra for brushing

1 tablespoon dark soy sauce

1/4 teaspoon salt

1/2 teaspoon ground black pepper

4–6 large green (spring) onions

MINTED COCONUT CHUTNEY

1 cup (1 1/2 oz/45 g) fresh mint leaves

1 onion

1/2 cup (1 oz/30 g) grated dried (desiccated) coconut

1/4 teaspoon black mustard seeds (optional)

1/4 cup (2 fl oz/60 ml) white vinegar

1 tablespoon sugar

Salt to taste

Place the meat in a large dish. Combine the onion, garlic, ginger, oil, soy sauce, salt, and pepper and mix well. Brush the meat with the mixture. Cover the meat with plastic wrap and set aside for 40 minutes.

Preheat a broiler (griller).

Cut the green onions into 1 1/4-inch (3-cm) lengths. Thread the meat pieces onto oiled metal skewers, alternating with the onion pieces. Brush with the extra oil and grill (broil), turning frequently, until done to your liking.

Meanwhile, for the chutney, in a food processor, finely chop the mint leaves; remove. Process the onion to a smooth paste, add the remaining ingredients and the chopped mint, and process until well mixed. Serve the kabobs accompanied with the mint chutney.

Serves 6

Margarita Steak with Grilled Onion Guacamole

MARINADE AND STEAK

1/3 cup (2 1/2 fl oz/80 ml) fresh lime juice

3 tablespoons olive oil

2 tablespoons tequila

2 tablespoons triple sec liqueur

2 teaspoons sugar

1 lb (500 g) top round steak, cut 1 inch (2.5 cm) thick

Salt and ground black pepper

GUACAMOLE

1 large red (Spanish) onion, cut into 1/2-inch (1-cm) thick slices

2 tablespoons extra virgin olive oil

2 ripe avocados, pitted and peeled

1 large clove garlic, minced

1 jalapeño chili, seeded and minced

4 teaspoons fresh lime juice

1 tablespoon chopped cilantro (fresh coriander)

1/2 teaspoon salt, plus more as needed

For the steak, in a shallow, nonreactive dish, whisk together the lime juice, olive oil, tequila, triple sec, and sugar. Add the steak and turn to coat. Cover and refrigerate for 4 hours, turning the steak once or twice.

Preheat a two-sided electric indoor grill (barbecue) or ridged grill pan according to the manufacturer's instructions.

Remove the steak from the marinade, shaking off the excess. Season it generously on both sides with salt and pepper.

If you are using the two-sided grill, coat the onions with oil, arrange them on the grill, close the cover, and cook until the onions are tender and charred, about 5 minutes. Set the onions aside to cool.

Place the steak on the grill, close the cover, and cook to the desired degree of doneness, 3–4 minutes for medium rare. Transfer to a cutting board and let stand for 5 minutes.

If you are using the grill pan, coat the onions with oil, then grill until tender and charred,

6–8 minutes, turning them once midway through cooking. Set them aside to cool.

Then cook the steak to the desired degree of doneness, 6–8 minutes for medium rare, turning it once midway through cooking. Transfer to a cutting board and let stand for 5 minutes.

While the steak is cooking, prepare the guacamole. Coarsely chop the grilled onions. In a mixing bowl, coarsely mash the avocados with a fork. Gently stir in the onions, garlic, jalapeño, lime juice, cilantro, and salt.

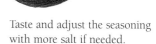

Taste and adjust the seasoning with more salt if needed.

To serve, thinly slice the meat across the grain, top with the guacamole, and serve at once.

Serves 4

Chicken with Kaffir Lime Leaves

2 oz (60 g) tamarind pulp, chopped

1 cup (8 fl oz/250 ml) boiling water

SPICE PASTE

1 x ½-inch (1-cm) piece fresh galangal, chopped; or 1 piece dried galangal (¼ inch/5 mm), soaked in water for 30 minutes then chopped

1 lemongrass stalk, tender heart section only, coarsely chopped

4 purple (Asia) shallots or 1 yellow onion, quartered

5 small red chilis, seeded

3 cloves garlic, peeled

1 teaspoon ground turmeric

About 3 tablespoons water

CHICKEN

¼ cup (2 fl oz/60 ml) canola oil

1 whole chicken, about 2 lb (1 kg), cut into serving pieces

1 cup (8 fl oz/250 ml) coconut milk

6 kaffir lime or other citrus leaves or the zest of 1 lime

1 teaspoon salt, or to taste

In a small bowl, soak the tamarind pulp in the boiling water for 15 minutes. Using the back of a fork, mash the tamarind to help dissolve the pulp. Pass it through a fine-mesh sieve into another small bowl, pressing against the pulp to

extract as much liquid as possible. Discard the pulp and reserve the tamarind liquid.

For the spice paste, in a blender or food processor, blend or process the galangal, lemongrass, shallots or onion, chilis, garlic, turmeric, and 3 tablespoons water to a smooth paste, adding more water if necessary.

In a large saucepan over medium heat, warm the oil. Add the spice paste and fry, stirring, until fragrant, thick, and creamy, about 3 minutes. Continue cooking, stirring, until the oil separates from the paste, about 5 minutes. Add the chicken pieces and fry, turning often,

until fully coated with the spice paste, about 3 minutes. Stir the reserved tamarind liquid into the pan and bring to a boil. Reduce the heat to medium and simmer, uncovered, turning occasionally, for 15 minutes. Add the coconut milk, lime or citrus leaves or zest, and salt. Simmer until the chicken is cooked through, about 10 minutes more. Serve hot.

Serves 4

Blackened Chicken

TOMATO-CHILI COULIS

1/3 cup (2 1/2 fl oz/80 ml) tomato paste

1 tomato, finely chopped

1 tablespoon fresh lime juice

1 tablespoon chili sauce

1/4 teaspoon Tabasco sauce

2 teaspoons chopped fresh dill

Salt and pepper to taste

6 skinless, boneless chicken breast halves (1 1/2 lb/750 g total)

1 tablespoon paprika

2 teaspoons black pepper

1/2 teaspoon cayenne pepper

2 teaspoons garlic powder

2 teaspoons onion powder

1 teaspoon salt

1 teaspoon dried thyme

1/2 cup (4 oz/125 g) olive oil

For the coulis, in a small bowl, mix the tomato paste, tomato, lime juice, chili sauce, Tabasco sauce, dill, and salt and pepper. Let stand for at least 1 hour.

Place each chicken breast half between 2 sheets of plastic wrap and, using the flat side of a meat mallet, pound the chicken until it is of uniform thickness.

In a screw-top jar, combine the paprika, black pepper, cayenne pepper, garlic powder, onion powder, salt, and thyme. Shake well to combine.

Preheat a broiler (griller) or heat grill (barbecue) to medium-high.

Dip the chicken into the olive oil and sprinkle both sides with the spice mixture. Place on a cooking rack. Broil (grill), 3 inches (7.5 cm) from heat, or grill (barbecue), until a black crust forms and the chicken is cooked through, 2 minutes on each side.

Serve the chicken with the tomato coulis.

Serves 6

Italian Sausage Casserole

1 lb (500 g) hot or mild Italian sausages

1 sweet onion such as Vidalia, cut into thin wedges

1/2 red bell pepper (capsicum), seeded and thickly sliced

1/2 teaspoon fennel seeds

1 small fennel bulb, trimmed and cut into thin wedges

1 medium zucchini (courgette), sliced

2 oz (60 g) fresh mushrooms, sliced

1 x 14-oz (440-g) can Italian-style whole tomatoes, undrained

1 tablespoon tomato paste

1 teaspoon sugar

Salt and ground black pepper

Shredded basil leaves, to serve

Cut the sausages into 1½-inch (4-cm) pieces. Heat a large frying pan, add the sausage, and cook, stirring, for 3–4 minutes, or until lightly browned. Remove and set aside.

Add the onion wedges, bell pepper, and fennel seeds to the pan juices in the frying pan. Cook for 2–3 minutes to soften a little. Place in the slow cooker (Dutch oven) along with the sausage, fennel wedges, zucchini, and mushrooms. Stir through the tomatoes and their juice, tomato paste, and sugar, and season to taste with salt and pepper.

Cover with the lid and cook on low for 5–6 hours. Sprinkle with shredded basil leaves and serve.

Serves 4 to 6

Spicy Grilled Snapper with Dill

1 or 2 snapper or bream (about 2 lb/1 kg total weight)

Salt and ground black pepper

2 tablespoons olive oil

1 lemon, sliced

3–4 fresh dill sprigs

Prepare a fire in a charcoal grill (barbecue) or preheat a broiler (griller).

Clean the fish and make several diagonal slashes on each side. Season inside and out with salt and pepper. On a piece of aluminum foil large enough to enclose the fish, brush the olive oil over an area the same size as the fish and place the fish on it. Place several lemon slices and a sprig or two of dill in the cavity of the fish and arrange the remaining lemon slices and herbs over the fish. Wrap the foil around the fish, folding the edges over to seal.

Grill (barbecue) or broil (grill) over medium heat until tender, about 25 minutes for 1 large fish and 15 minutes for 2 smaller fish. Test by inserting a skewer into the thickest part of the fish; if the flesh is tender and white, the fish is done. Serve hot.

Serves 4

Saffron Mussel Stew

2 tablespoons olive oil

2 yellow onions, cut into julienne strips

1/2 teaspoon salt

1/2 teaspoon ground black pepper

4 cloves garlic, sliced

1 1/2 cups (12 fl oz/375 ml) dry white wine

1 fresh thyme sprig

1 teaspoon saffron threads

2 1/2 cups (20 fl oz/600 ml) bottled clam juice or fish stock

1 cup (8 fl oz/250 ml) good-quality tomato juice

3 lb (1.5 kg) small mussels in the shells

1/2 cup (3/4 oz/20 g) coarsely chopped fresh flat-leaf (Italian) parsley

Heat 1 tablespoon of the olive oil in a large, heavy based saucepan over medium heat. Add half of the onion, the salt, and pepper. Cook, stirring often, until the onion is light golden, 8–10 minutes. Add the garlic and stir for 1 minute. Stir in the wine and bring to a boil. Boil until the mixture has reduced by half, about 8 minutes. Stir in the thyme, saffron, clam juice or fish stock, and tomato juice and bring

to a boil. Reduce the heat to low and simmer for 10 minutes to blend the flavors. Strain the broth and discard the solids. Set aside.

Scrub the mussels under cold, running water and remove the beards. Discard any mussels that do not close when lightly touched.

Place 2 large frying pans over high heat (or cook in batches if only 1 pan is available).

Add 2 teaspoons of the remaining olive oil to each pan. When the oil is hot, add half of the remaining onions to each pan and cook, stirring occasionally, until they just begin

to color, about 4 minutes. Add half of the mussels to each pan, spreading them out in a single layer, and cook, stirring occasionally, for 2 minutes. Divide the strained broth between the pans and bring to a boil. Reduce the heat to medium, cover, and cook until the mussels open, 3–5 minutes. Discard any mussels that do not open.

Add half of the parsley to each pan. Toss to combine and then spoon the mussels into warmed serving dishes. Divide the broth among the bowls and serve immediately, while hot.

Serves 4

Chicken with Straw Mushrooms

MARINADE

1 tablespoon light soy sauce

1 teaspoon dark soy sauce

1 teaspoon sugar

1½ lb (750 g) chicken breast meat, cut into finger-size strips

1 cup (8 fl oz/250 ml) peanut oil

3–4 slices peeled fresh ginger

12 dried straw mushrooms, soaked in warm water for 1 hour to soften, drained

1 cup (8 oz/250 g) cauliflower florets, blanched

2 spring (green) onions, cut into 1-inch (2.5-cm) lengths

1½ teaspoons salt

1 teaspoon sugar

½ cup (4 fl oz/125 ml) chicken stock

1 teaspoon rice wine

For the marinade, in a bowl, combine the soy sauces and sugar. Mix well. Add the chicken and coat with the marinade. Cover and marinate for 30 minutes.

In a wok or large frying pan over high heat, warm the oil. Add the chicken and stir-fry until it turns white, about 45 seconds. Remove the chicken from the wok and drain on paper towels.

Drain all but 1–2 tablespoons of oil from the wok and warm over high heat. Add the ginger and mushrooms and stir-fry for about 30 seconds. Add the cauliflower and stir.

Return the chicken to the wok and stir-fry for a further 30 seconds. Add the green onions, salt, sugar, and stock. Stir well. Add the rice wine and serve immediately.

Serves 4 to 6

Stewed Clams, Sausage, and Tomatoes

2½ lb (1.25 kg) small clams in the shell

2 tablespoons olive oil

3 yellow or red (Spanish) onions, thinly sliced

4 cloves garlic, minced

1½ tablespoons dried chili flakes or 2 small fresh red chilis, seeded and minced (optional)

1 bay leaf, crumbled

4 oz (125 g) smoked ham or prosciutto, diced

4 oz (125 g) chorizo or other spicy sausage, casing removed, crumbled

½ cup (4 fl oz/125 ml) dry white wine

1 can (12 oz/375 g) chopped tomatoes

½ cup (¾ oz/20 g) chopped fresh flat-leaf (Italian) parsley

Ground black pepper

Lemon wedges

CHILI SAUCE

½ cup (2 oz/60 g) coarsely chopped fresh red chilis

3 cloves garlic, minced

1 teaspoon coarse (kosher) salt

1 cup (8 fl oz/250 ml) olive oil

¼ cup (2 fl oz/60 ml) red wine vinegar (optional)

Discard any clams that do not close when lightly touched. Scrub the clams under cold, running water. Place clams in a bowl of water, and refrigerate until needed.

Heat the oil in a large saucepan over medium heat. Add the onions and cook, stirring often, until tender, about 15 minutes. Add the garlic and chili flakes (if using) and stir for 3 minutes. Add the fresh chilis (if using), the bay leaf, ham or prosciutto, chorizo or other sausage, wine, and tomatoes. Stir well and simmer, uncovered, over low heat for 25 minutes.

Add the clams, hinges down, and cover the pan. Increase the heat to high and cook until the clams open, 3–5 minutes. Discard any that do not open.

For the chili sauce, combine all ingredients in a jar. Cover and leave in a cool, dark place for at least 1 week or up to 1 month. Shake well before using.

Sprinkle the clams with parsley and plenty of black pepper. Serve hot, with lemon wedges and the chili sauce.

Serves 4

SIDE DISHES

Asparagus with Orange-Sesame Dressing

FOR THE DRESSING

2 teaspoons sesame seeds

¼ cup (2 fl oz/60 ml) orange juice

¼ teaspoon sugar

1 teaspoon olive oil

1 teaspoon toasted (Asian) sesame oil

¼ teaspoon grated orange zest

FOR THE ASPARAGUS

1 lb (500 g) fresh asparagus

2 teaspoons extra virgin olive oil

½ teaspoon salt

¼ teaspoon ground black pepper

To make the dressing, in a small saucepan stir the sesame seeds constantly over medium heat until deeply golden and fragrant, about 4 minutes; transfer them to a small saucer to cool.

Add the orange juice and sugar to the pan; increase the heat to high and cook, swirling the pan, until the juice has thickened and reduced to 1 tablespoon, about 3 minutes. Whisk in the olive and sesame oils, orange zest, and sesame seeds. Set aside.

To prepare the asparagus, snap off the woody bottom of each spear at the point near the base where the stalk begins to bend. With a vegetable peeler, remove the skin from the stalk by scraping from just below the tip toward the base.

In a shallow dish, gently toss the peeled asparagus with the olive oil, salt, and pepper.

Preheat a large two-sided electric indoor grill (barbecue) or ridged grill pan according to the manufacturer's instructions.

If you are using the two-sided grill, arrange the asparagus in a single layer, close the cover, and cook until just tender, about 8 minutes.

If you are using the grill pan, cook the asparagus until just tender, about 10 minutes, turning it several times.

Serve the asparagus hot or at room temperature, drizzled with the dressing.

Serves 4

Sautéed Mushrooms with Garlic

1/3 cup (2 1/2 fl oz/80 ml) olive oil

2 tablespoons minced garlic

1/4 cup (1 1/2 oz/45 g) diced bacon or cooked diced ham

1 lb (500 g) fresh mushrooms (see note), brushed clean and halved if small, or sliced 1/4 inch (6 mm) thick

1/2 cup (4 fl oz/125 ml) dry white wine or dry sherry, if needed

1/3 cup (1/2 oz/15 g) chopped fresh flat-leaf (Italian) parsley, or 1/4 cup (1/3 oz/10 g) chopped fresh flat-leaf (Italian) parsley and 2 tablespoons chopped fresh thyme

Salt and ground black pepper

In a large frying pan over medium heat, warm the olive oil. Add the garlic and bacon or ham and sauté for 2 minutes. Raise the heat to high, add the mushrooms, and continue to sauté, stirring briskly, until they release their juices and the liquid evaporates, 5–8 minutes.

If the mushrooms do not release much liquid, add the wine and cook until the liquid evaporates.

Add the parsley (and thyme, if using) and stir. Season with salt and pepper and serve hot.

Serves 4

NOTE Savor these garlicky sautéed mushrooms hot from the pan. Spoon them over toast as a snack, or alongside grilled (barbecued) lamb, beef, or chicken as a flavorful side dish. For a particularly delicious variation, combine chanterelles, portobellos, and cremini with the more common white mushrooms.

Eggplant in Spicy Sauce

4 medium eggplants (aubergines)

3 tablespoons peanut oil

8 oz (250 g) ground (minced) pork

2 tablespoons peeled, minced fresh ginger

6 large cloves garlic, minced

2 green (spring) onions, chopped

1 teaspoon hot chili bean paste

SEASONINGS

1/2 cup (4 fl oz/125 ml) chicken stock

3 tablespoons light soy sauce

1/4 teaspoon ground white pepper

1 teaspoon sugar (optional)

1 tablespoon cornstarch (cornflour), mixed with a little cold water

Slice the eggplants in half crosswise and then into thick finger-length pieces.

Bring a large saucepan of water to a boil. Add the eggplant and quickly return to a boil. Drain immediately and refresh in cold water. (The eggplant should still be firm, not mushy.) Transfer to a plate and set aside.

Preheat a wok or large frying pan over medium-high heat. Add the peanut oil and heat until it reaches smoking point.

Add the ground pork and stir-fry until it changes color. Add the ginger, garlic, and green onion and stir-fry until fragrant. Add the hot chili bean paste and mix through. Add the eggplant and toss quickly over high heat. Add all of the seasonings and cook, stirring constantly, until the sauce thickens and coats the pieces. Serve hot.

Serves 8

Garlic Green Beans

1 tablespoon peanut oil

10 large cloves garlic, peeled

2 cups (16 fl oz/500 ml) chicken stock

1 lb (500 g) green beans, topped and tailed

½ tablespoon cornstarch (cornflour), mixed with 2 tablespoons cold water, for thickening

In a large frying pan, combine the oil and whole garlic cloves. Stir over medium heat until the garlic is lightly golden, about 2 minutes. Add the stock, cover, and simmer until the garlic is tender when pierced, 5 minutes.

Bring the stock back to a boil and add the beans. Cook, covered, just until the beans are crisp-tender, 3–4 minutes. With tongs, lift out the beans and arrange on a serving plate.

Stir the cornstarch mixture into the stock in the frying pan. Bring to a boil, stirring until thickened. Spoon the sauce and garlic over the beans. Serve hot.

Serves 6

Greek Salad

DRESSING

½ cup (4 fl oz/125 ml) extra virgin olive oil

2–3 tablespoons fresh lemon juice

3 tablespoons dried oregano

Cracked black pepper

1 clove garlic, minced (optional)

2–3 cups (2–3 oz/60–100 g) torn assorted salad greens such as romaine (cos) lettuce, escarole (curly endive/chicory), or frisée

4 small ripe tomatoes, cored and cut into wedges

1 large cucumber, peeled, seeded, and cut into wedges

1 red (Spanish) onion, thinly sliced into rings

2 small green bell peppers (capsicums), seeded, deribbed, and thinly sliced crosswise into rings

8 oz (250 g) feta cheese, coarsely crumbled

20 Kalamata olives

To make the dressing, in a bowl, stir together the olive oil, lemon juice, oregano, cracked pepper to taste, and the garlic, if using. Set aside.

In a large salad bowl, combine the greens, tomatoes, cucumber, onion, and bell peppers. Drizzle the dressing over the top and toss gently to mix. Sprinkle the feta cheese and olives over the top and serve at once.

Serves 4

Tomato, Mozzarella, and Basil Salad

12 oz (375 g) fresh mozzarella cheese, drained

1/4 cup (2 fl oz/60 ml) extra virgin olive oil

Salt and pepper

12 fresh basil leaves, thinly sliced

2 tablespoons coarsely chopped fresh flat-leaf (Italian) parsley

12 oz (375 g) round and/or pear-shaped (teardrop) cherry tomatoes, in a mixture of colors

2 stalks celery, sliced on the diagonal

1/4 cup (1 1/2 oz/45 g) Moroccan olives or other oil-cured olives

If using large balls of mozzarella, cut them into 1/2-inch (1-cm) dice. If using smaller balls, cut them into fourths. In a bowl, toss the mozzarella with half of the olive oil and salt and pepper to taste. Add half of the basil and half of the parsley. Toss gently.

If using round cherry tomatoes, cut them in halves. If using pear-shaped ones, leave them whole. In another bowl, combine the tomatoes and celery with the remaining olive oil and salt and pepper to taste. Toss gently.

Mound the mozzarella in the center of individual plates. Make a ring of the seasoned tomatoes and celery around the edge and garnish with the olives. Serve immediately.

Serves 4 to 6

Tricolor Coleslaw

DRESSING

3 tablespoons cider vinegar

1/2 tablespoon sugar

2 cups (16 fl oz/500 ml) mayonnaise

1/4 teaspoon salt

1/4 teaspoon ground black pepper

3 tablespoons finely chopped fresh parsley

SALAD

1/2 small head red cabbage, shredded (about 3 cups/9 oz/ 275 g)

1 small head green cabbage, shredded (about 5 cups/15 oz/ 470 g)

2 carrots, peeled and shredded (about 1 cup/5 oz/155 g)

To make the dressing, in a large serving bowl, stir together the vinegar, sugar, mayonnaise, salt, pepper, and parsley until they are well blended.

Add the cabbage and carrot to the dressing. Using tongs, toss to coat all the vegetables evenly with the dressing.

Cover with plastic wrap and chill for at least 2 hours and up to 8 hours before serving.

Serves 6 to 8

Slow-Cooked Vegetable Casserole

3 tablespoons olive oil

1 medium sweet onion, such as Vidalia, cut into thin wedges

3 cloves garlic, minced

1 lb (500 g) eggplant (aubergine), cut into chunks

2 medium zucchini (courgettes), cut into 1-inch (2.5-cm) thick slices

1 stalk celery, cut into 1-inch (2.5-cm) thick slices

1 red bell pepper (capsicum), seeded and cut into 1-inch (2.5-cm) chunks

1 lb (500 g) ripe tomatoes, peeled, seeded, and chopped

1 tablespoon tomato paste

1 teaspoon sugar (optional)

2 sprigs fresh thyme

Salt and ground black pepper

Extra fresh thyme leaves, for sprinkling

2 tablespoons capers

Heat the oil in a large frying pan over medium heat and cook the onion and garlic for 2–3 minutes. Add the eggplant and cook, stirring, over medium-high heat for 4–5 minutes, or until the eggplant is lightly browned.

Transfer to a slow cooker. Stir in the zucchini, celery, bell pepper, chopped tomatoes, tomato paste, sugar, and thyme sprigs. Season to taste with salt and pepper.

Put on the lid and cook on Low for 6–8 hours. The vegetables should be soft, but not mushy. Remove the thyme sprigs and sprinkle with the extra fresh thyme leaves and capers. Serve warm or at room temperature.

Serves 4 to 6

Vegetable Terrine with Tomato Sauce

TOMATO LAYER

1/4 cup (2 fl oz/60 ml) olive oil

2 yellow onions, finely chopped

4 medium tomatoes, peeled, seeded, and chopped

2 cloves garlic, minced

2 tablespoons chopped basil

3 tablespoons tomato paste

1 teaspoon chili powder

Salt and ground black pepper

1 whole egg, plus 1 egg yolk

LEEK LAYER

1/3 cup (2 1/2 fl oz/80 ml) olive oil

3 leeks, thinly sliced

2 cloves garlic, minced

1/2 cup (1/2 oz/15 g) chopped parsley

Salt and ground black pepper

1 whole egg, plus 1 egg yolk

TO ASSEMBLE

12 large cabbage leaves, blanched briefly in boiling water and refreshed in cold water

1 bunch asparagus, blanched briefly in boiling water and refreshed in cold water

2 red bell peppers (capsicums), roasted, skinned, and seeded

6 yellow squash, thinly sliced, blanched briefly in boiling water, and refreshed in cold water

TOMATO SAUCE

5 medium tomatoes, peeled and seeded

2 tablespoons red wine vinegar

Dash of hot-pepper sauce

1/2 teaspoon chili powder (optional)

Salt and ground black pepper

1/3 cup (2 1/2 fl oz/80 ml) olive oil

For the tomato layer, heat the olive oil in a large, heavy-based, nonreactive pan. Add the onion, cover, and cook on low heat for 20 minutes. Drain the tomatoes and add to the onion. Cook, stirring often, for 20 minutes. Add the garlic, basil, tomato paste, chili powder, and salt and pepper to taste, and cook for 15 minutes, or until the mixture is very thick. Cool to room temperature. Whisk the egg and egg yolk into the tomato mixture. Cover and refrigerate until very cool. (This can be done up to a day ahead.)

For the leek layer, heat the olive oil in a heavy-based pan. Add the leeks, cover, and cook on low heat for 30 minutes—do not let the leeks brown. Add the garlic, parsley, and salt and pepper to taste, and cook, uncovered, for another 10 minutes. Cool to room temperature. Beat the egg and yolk together in a small bowl. Stir into the leek mixture. Cover and refrigerate until very cool. (This can be done up to a day ahead.)

Preheat the oven to 375°F (190°C/Gas Mark 4). To assemble the terrine, drain the cabbage, asparagus, bell peppers, and squash; pat dry with paper towels. Lightly butter a 9- x 5- x 3-inch (23- x 13- x 7.5-cm) terrine or loaf pan. Trim the heavy ribs from the cabbage

leaves. Line the pan with cabbage leaves, overlapping them and allowing the tops to hang out over the edges of the pan. Reserve 2 or 3 cabbage leaves for the top.

Stir the cooled leek and tomato mixtures. Smooth half of the tomato mixture on the bottom of the lined terrine. Layer the asparagus on top, then add all of the leek mixture, smoothing the surface. Layer the roasted bell peppers on top and cover with the rest of the tomato mixture. Arrange the squash slices on top. Fold the over-hanging cabbage leaves over the top, tucking any excess down the sides of the terrine.

VEGETABLE TERRINE WITH TOMATO SAUCE

Wrap the terrine in aluminum foil, place in a large baking pan, and pour in boiling water to reach halfway up the sides of the terrine. Bake in the center of the oven for 2 hours, or until the terrine is firm to the touch. Remove from the water and unwrap. Cool for 15 minutes. Set a weight over the terrine and cool completely. Remove the weight, cover the terrine, and refrigerate. To unmold, dip the pan briefly in hot water and run a thin knife around the sides, then invert. Serve with tomato sauce.

While the terrine is baking, make the tomato sauce. Process all the ingredients, except the oil, together in a food processor until smooth. Add the oil in a slow, steady stream and process until completely combined. Chill in the refrigerator. Adjust seasoning just before serving.

Serves 6

Caponata

3 tablespoons olive oil

1 sweet white onion, such as Vidalia, cut into thin wedges

3 cloves garlic, peeled and thinly sliced

1 stalk celery, cut into 1-inch (2.5-cm) slices

2 red bell peppers (capsicums), seeded and cut into 1-inch (2.5-cm) pieces

1 medium eggplant (aubergine), cut into 1-inch (2.5-cm) cubes

1 can (14 oz/440 g) chopped tomatoes

1 tablespoon tomato paste

2 tablespoons red wine vinegar

1/2 tablespoon brown sugar (optional)

Salt and ground black pepper

10 black olives, pitted and chopped

2 tablespoons capers

Heat the oil in a large frying pan and cook the onion, garlic, and celery for 2–3 minutes. Add the red bell pepper and eggplant, stir, and cook on medium heat for 15 minutes, or until the eggplant is lightly browned.

Stir in the tomatoes, tomato paste, vinegar, and sugar. Season to taste with salt and pepper.

Cook, uncovered, over low heat for 15 minutes until the vegetables are soft, but not mushy. Stir in the olives and capers. Serve the caponata warm or at room temperature.

Serves 4 to 6

Asparagus with Olive Oil and Parmesan

2 bunches (1½ lb/750 g) asparagus, trimmed

⅓ cup (2½ fl oz/80 ml) olive oil, plus extra to serve

6 oz (190 g) Parmesan cheese, shaved, plus extra to serve

Ground black pepper

Steam the asparagus for about 12 minutes, or microwave the asparagus on High (100%) for 5–7 minutes, or until tender.

Place the asparagus on a large platter, drizzle with the olive oil, and sprinkle with the Parmesan and pepper to taste.

Serve with extra Parmesan, pepper, and olive oil.

Serves 4

Chinese Cabbage with Sesame Seeds

2 tablespoons sesame seeds

1½ cups (12 fl oz/375 ml) vegetable stock

4 green (spring) onions

1 small head Chinese (napa) cabbage, thinly sliced lengthwise and then cut in half crosswise

2 tablespoons peanut oil

½ teaspoon crushed dried chilies

Salt and ground white pepper

Toast the sesame seeds in a small, dry frying pan over medium-low heat, stirring, for 2–3 minutes, or until lightly colored. Set aside.

Pour the stock into a large frying pan over high heat and boil for 2–3 minutes, or until the stock is slightly reduced.

Cut the green onions in half lengthwise, then cut into long, thin strips. Add to the boiling stock.

Add the cabbage and reduce the heat to medium. Cook, stirring occasionally, until tender, about 5 minutes. The stock should be almost totally absorbed.

Stir in the oil, sesame seeds, crushed dried chilies, and salt and pepper to taste. Serve hot.

Serves 4

Italian Broccoli with Olives

3 or 4 broccoli stalks, about
1 lb (500 g)

3 tablespoons olive oil

1 tablespoon red wine vinegar

Juice of 1/2 lemon

Salt and ground pepper

1 tablespoon capers

1/2 cup (2 1/2 oz/80 g) pitted black
olives, chopped

Trim the broccoli stalks and discard the coarse leaves; pare stems to remove coarse skin, if desired. Split each broccoli stalk lengthwise into thin spears (the number depends upon the thickness of the stalks).

Fill a saucepan with just enough water to cover the broccoli once it is added. Bring to a boil. Add the broccoli and cook, uncovered, over high heat for 4–5 minutes, or until tender but firm. (If cooked quickly, broccoli will retain its bright color.) Drain and place in a serving dish. Immediately pour the olive oil over the broccoli, add the vinegar, and carefully toss. Add the lemon juice and season to taste with salt and pepper.

Toss again. Add the capers and olives, turning the broccoli gently until thoroughly combined. Serve at room temperature.

Serves 4

Tomato, Prosciutto, and Mozzarella Salad with Balsamic Vinaigrette

10 oz (300 g) plum (Roma) tomatoes

5 oz (160 g) yellow pear-shaped cherry tomatoes

6 oz (190 g) cherry tomatoes

8 oz (250 g) small fresh mozzarella (bocconcini)

3½ oz (105 g) finely sliced prosciutto

1 cup (1 oz /30 g) basil leaves, torn if large

DRESSING

½ cup (4 fl oz/125 ml) extra virgin olive oil

2 tablespoons balsamic vinegar

Salt and ground pepper

For the dressing, whisk together the olive oil and balsamic vinegar until well blended. Add salt and pepper to taste.

Slice the plum tomatoes into rounds. Halve all the cherry tomatoes. Slice the fresh mozzarella (bocconcini).

Arrange the salad ingredients on 4 individual serving plates. Drizzle some of the dressing over each salad. Serve the salad at room temperature.

Serves 4

Stir-Fried Green Vegetables

1/4 cup (2 fl oz/60 ml) canola oil

3 stalks celery, trimmed and cut on the diagonal

8 oz (250 g) green beans, trimmed and cut on the diagonal

6 cauliflower florets, cut on the diagonal

6 broccoli florets, cut on the diagonal

1 small head bok choy, leaves cut into long, thin slivers

1 cup (8 fl oz/250 ml) vegetable stock, heated

1 tablespoon soy sauce

1/2 teaspoon crushed dried chilies

1/2 cup (3 oz/100 g) almonds, coarsely chopped, or pine nuts

Heat the oil in a large wok or frying pan over medium-high heat. Add the celery, beans, cauliflower, broccoli, and bok choy and stir until evenly coated with the oil.

Raise the heat to high and add 1/2 cup (4 fl oz/125 ml) of the stock, the soy sauce, and the chilis. Cook, stirring constantly, for 2–4 minutes, or until the vegetables are just tender, or done to your liking.

As the stock evaporates, add only enough of the remaining stock to prevent sticking.

Taste and adjust the seasoning with more soy sauce and/or chilies. Stir in the almonds and serve immediately.

Serves 4 to 6

About Almonds

The almond tree has been valued for its nutritious nut for thousands of years. Not surprisingly, the delicately flavored almond turns up in all courses—from roasted and salted as a snack to an ingredient in the most elegant dessert—in most of the world's cuisines.

Storing Almonds are sold whole, roasted, salted, blanched, halved, slivered, flaked, chopped, ground, or in the form of a paste. They keep best in their shells, but as they are readily available year-round, you may prefer to buy them as you need them and in the form you need them for particular purposes. For example, buy only small quantities of ground almonds, or almond meal, for cakes and cookies and use quickly. You can buy larger quantities of whole, unblanched almonds, which are protected by their skins. Always store in an airtight container in the refrigerator or some other cool place.

To Blanch Almonds Place nuts in a bowl, pour on enough boiling water to cover generously and stand for 5 minutes. Drain and rinse with cold water. As you press each kernel between your thumb and forefinger, the brown skin will slip off easily. Dry the kernels on a clean tea towel before use.

Pear, Walnut, and Blue Cheese Salad

6 pears

4 cups (3 oz/100 g) mixed salad leaves, such as escarole (curly endive/chicory), watercress, baby spinach, arugula (rocket), and snow pea (mangetout) sprouts

3 stalks celery, sliced

DRESSING

1/4 cup (2 fl oz/60 ml) walnut oil

1/4 cup (2 fl oz/60 ml) safflower or olive oil

2 tablespoons lemon juice

2 tablespoons snipped chives

1/2 cup (4 oz/125 g) crumbled blue cheese

1/2 cup (2 oz/60 g) walnuts, chopped

Slice the pears into thin wedges. Arrange the pear wedges and salad leaves in individual bowls. Scatter an equal amount of celery in each bowl.

For the dressing, combine the oils and lemon juice, and pour over the salads.

Sprinkle the chives, cheese, and walnuts on top of each salad and serve.

Serves 6

Grilled Vegetable Salad

2 red (Spanish) onions, unpeeled

1/4 cup (2 fl oz/60 ml) red wine vinegar

1 teaspoon salt, or to taste

1/2 teaspoon ground pepper

3 tablespoons coarsely chopped fresh oregano or marjoram

1 large clove garlic, minced

2/3 cup (5 fl oz/160 ml) olive oil

1 medium or 2 small Asian (slender) eggplants (aubergines)

1 zucchini (courgette)

1 yellow crookneck squash

1 bulb fennel

1 large red bell pepper (capsicum), seeded, deribbed, and quartered lengthwise

GRILLED VEGETABLE SALAD

Preheat a broiler (griller) or prepare a fire in a charcoal grill (barbecue).

If using a broiler, place the unpeeled onions in a small baking pan and cover with aluminum foil. Place the pan in the broiler or place the onions directly on the grill rack about 5 inches (13 cm) from the heat source. Broil (grill) or grill (barbecue), turning every 5–10 minutes, until charred on the outside and soft throughout, about 1 hour if using a broiler or 20–30 minutes if using a grill. Remove from the broiler or grill; set aside to cool slightly.

Meanwhile, in a small bowl, whisk together the vinegar, salt, pepper, oregano or marjoram, and garlic. Slowly add the olive oil, whisking constantly.

Trim the ends from the eggplant, zucchini, and squash, and any stalks from the fennel bulb and slice lengthwise. Place in a bowl with the bell pepper and half of the vinaigrette and toss to coat the vegetables. Arrange them on a broiler pan or directly on a grill rack about 5 inches (13 cm) from the heat source. Broil (grill) or grill (barbecue) slowly, turning to cook evenly, for 5–10 minutes

for the squash, peppers, and eggplants, and 15 minutes for the fennel, or until the vegetables are lightly golden and cooked through. Remove from the broiler or grill rack and let cool.

Peel the onions and cut each into 8 wedges. Place in a bowl. Cut all the remaining vegetables into 2-inch (5-cm) pieces as well and add to the bowl. Pour the remaining vinaigrette over the vegetables and toss to coat.

Spoon the vegetables on to individual plates and serve.

Serves 4 to 6

Summer Ratatouille

1 small eggplant (aubergine), about 1 lb (500 g)

1/4 cup (2 fl oz/60 ml) olive oil

1 red (Spanish) onion, thinly sliced

1 yellow or red bell pepper (capsicum), seeded, deribbed, and sliced lengthwise

2 cloves garlic, cut in half

2 large ripe tomatoes, sliced

1 teaspoon dried thyme

1 teaspoon dried oregano

1/4 cup (2 fl oz/60 ml) vegetable stock

Salt and ground pepper

Cut the unpeeled eggplant lengthwise into fourths, then cut each piece into long, thin strips. Set aside.

Heat the olive oil in a large frying pan over medium heat. Add the onion and cook for about 5 minutes, or until soft. Add the bell pepper, garlic, and tomatoes and stir well. Mix in the thyme and oregano.

Add the eggplant to the pan along with the vegetable stock. Cover and simmer over low heat, stirring occasionally to prevent sticking, for about 20–30 minutes, or until the vegetables are soft. Discard the garlic halves. Season to taste with salt and pepper.

Transfer to a serving dish and serve hot, or at room temperature.

Serves 4

Prosciutto, Pear, and Parmesan Salad

DRESSING

3 tablespoons extra virgin olive oil

1 tablespoon balsamic vinegar

Juice of 1 lemon

1 tablespoon finely chopped chervil

1 clove garlic, minced

Salt and ground pepper

1 bunch (3½ oz/105 g) arugula (rocket)

4 medium-size ripe pears

Juice of 1 lemon

3½ oz (105 g) thinly sliced prosciutto

3½ oz (105 g) grated Parmesan cheese

2 tablespoons small chervil sprigs

Ground black pepper

For the dressing, combine all of the ingredients in a small bowl and whisk until well blended.

Arrange the arugula leaves in individual serving bowls. Drizzle with a little of the dressing and toss gently.

Leaving the skin on, cut each pear into 8 pieces. Sprinkle the pear pieces with the lemon juice to prevent discoloration. Tear the prosciutto into bite-size pieces. Arrange the pears and prosciutto over the arugula. Scatter the Parmesan and chervil sprigs on top. Drizzle with more dressing. Add ground black pepper to taste and serve.

Serves 4

Summer Vegetable Salad

1½ lb (750 g) broccoli, cut into small florets

11 oz (345 g) baby squash, halved or quartered

2 carrots, peeled and cut into thick matchsticks

1 red bell pepper (capsicum), cut into strips

1 small avocado, cut into chunks

3½ oz (105 g) sugar snap peas

MUSTARD SEED VINAIGRETTE

1½ tablespoons grain mustard

¼ cup (2 fl oz/60 ml) tarragon vinegar

Salt and ground black pepper

¾ cup (6 fl oz/190 ml) extra virgin olive oil

Bring a large saucepan of salted water to a boil. Add the broccoli, bring back to a boil, and simmer over medium heat for about 5 minutes, or until the broccoli is tender. Drain and refresh in cold water. Repeat with the squash, shortening the cooking time. Place the carrots in a saucepan, cover with cold water, bring to a boil, and simmer over medium heat for several minutes, or until tender. Refresh in cold water. Combine all the vegetables in a bowl.

For the dressing, whisk the mustard in a small bowl with the vinegar, and salt and pepper to taste. Slowly add the olive oil, whisking constantly until the dressing is foamy. Pour the dressing over the vegetables and toss to coat well. Serve.

Serves 4 to 6

Warm Mixed Mushroom and Asparagus Salad

3½ oz (105 g) shiitake mushrooms

5 oz (160 g) button mushrooms

5 oz (160 g) oyster mushrooms

1 bunch (5 oz/160 g) asparagus

¼ cup (2 fl oz/60 ml) walnut oil

Salt and ground pepper

1 bunch (3½ oz/105 g) watercress, washed and dried

2 tablespoons raspberry vinegar

Clean the mushrooms with a damp cloth. Halve any large ones. Cut the asparagus into 2-inch (5-cm) lengths. Cook the asparagus in boiling, salted water until just tender. Plunge into cold water. Drain.

Heat the walnut oil in a large wok or frying pan. Add the button and shiitake mushrooms and stir-fry for 2 minutes. Add the oyster mushrooms and stir-fry for 2 minutes. Add the asparagus and stir to combine. Season with salt and ground black pepper.

Arrange the watercress on a serving plate. Pile the mushrooms and asparagus in the center.

Bring the raspberry vinegar to a boil in the pan used for the mushrooms. Pour the vinegar over the salad and serve.

Serves 4 to 6

Baby Squash and Yellow Pepper Salad with Raspberry Vinaigrette

---

10 oz (300 g) mixed yellow and green baby squash

2 yellow bell peppers (capsicums)

a few sprigs chervil, to garnish

DRESSING

2 tablespoons raspberry vinegar

¼ cup (2 fl oz /60 ml) olive oil

2 teaspoons Dijon mustard

¼ teaspoon salt

Bring a large saucepan of salted water to a boil. Add the squash. When the water returns to a full boil remove from the heat, drain the squash, and plunge them into cold water for 3 minutes. Drain and set aside.

Halve the peppers and remove the seeds and membrane. Place under the broiler (griller), and cook until their skins are blackened. Place the peppers in a plastic bag and seal. Let cool. When cool, remove the skins from the peppers and cut them

into thin strips. Slice the squash finely and arrange it decoratively in rows on a serving plate. Arrange strips of peppers between the rows.

For the dressing, combine all of the ingredients in a small bowl. Whisk until well combined. Drizzle the dressing over the salad and set aside for at least 30 minutes to allow the flavors to develop. Garnish with chervil and serve.

Serves 4

Roasted Tomato Salad

1¾ lb (800 g) large tomatoes

1 bunch green (spring) onions

6 garlic cloves, peeled

5 tablespoons extra virgin olive oil

1 tablespoon fresh thyme leaves

Ground black pepper

1 tablespoon balsamic vinegar

1 tablespoon finely chopped fresh flat-leaf (Italian) parsley

Peel the tomatoes by covering them with boiling water for about 20 seconds then plunging then into cold water. Drain and carefully remove the skins. Halve the skinned tomatoes and squeeze out the seeds. Allow to drain for 30 minutes on a wire rack.

Preheat an oven to 375°F (190°C/Gas Mark 4). Arrange the tomatoes, cut sides up, in a shallow baking dish. Halve the green (spring) onions and garlic cloves and add to the dish. Pour on the oil and scatter with thyme and pepper. Bake, uncovered, for 30 minutes. Remove from the oven and let cool. When the tomatoes are cool enough to

handle, arrange them, cut side down, on a serving plate. Spoon on the green onions and garlic. Whisk the balsamic vinegar into the oil that remains in the baking dish. Drizzle the mixture over the tomatoes and onions. Sprinkle with the parsley. Serve warm or at room temperature. This salad makes a good accompaniment to roasted and broiled (grilled) meat.

Serves 4 to 6

Cauliflower with Garlic and Paprika

1½ lb (750 g) cauliflower, cut into florets

1 teaspoon lemon juice or white wine vinegar

¼ cup (2 fl oz/60 ml) olive oil

2 thick slices French bread (about 2 oz/60 g)

2 teaspoons paprika

1⅔ cups (13 fl oz/410 ml) water for cooking

Salt

1½ tablespoons finely chopped parsley

2 cloves garlic, peeled

2 teaspoons pine nuts

Rinse the cauliflower and place it in a bowl of water with the lemon juice or vinegar.

Heat the oil in a heatproof casserole and fry the bread slices. Remove and set aside. Reduce the heat and add the paprika.

Stir, then quickly pour in the water. Increase the heat. When the water comes to a boil, add the cauliflower florets and a little salt. Cook, uncovered, over medium heat for 15–20 minutes.

Crush the parsley, garlic, fried bread, and pine nuts in a mortar. When the ingredients are mixed thoroughly, add a little of the cooking water from the cauliflower, stir, then pour into the casserole. Adjust the seasoning to taste.

Cook for a further 5 minutes, then serve.

Serves 4

Okra with Tomatoes

3 tablespoons olive oil

I yellow onion, chopped

I clove garlic, cut in half

I teaspoon dried rosemary

I lb (500 g) okra, stemmed and thinly sliced crosswise (about 3 cups)

I cup (8 fl oz/250 ml) tomato sauce, purchased or home-made

4 tomatoes, coarsely chopped

I bay leaf

1/4 teaspoon crushed dried chilies

Salt and ground pepper

2 tablespoons chopped fresh parsley

Warm the oil in a frying pan over medium heat. Add the onion and cook for about 2 minutes, or until soft. Add the garlic and cook for about 1 minute longer, or until soft. Add the rosemary and okra and stir until coated thoroughly with the oil. Stir in the tomato sauce. Add the tomatoes, bay leaf, and crushed dried chilies. Simmer, uncovered, over medium heat for 10–15 minutes, or until the okra is tender.

Season to taste with salt and pepper. Discard the bay leaf and garlic halves. Serve hot or warm, garnished with the parsley.

Serves 4

Tomato and Zucchini Gratin

1/3 cup (2 1/2 fl oz/80 ml) olive oil

2 white onions, thinly sliced

2 cloves garlic, minced

1 red bell pepper (capsicum), seeded and cut into thin strips

1 green bell pepper (capsicum), seeded and cut into thin strips

1 lb (500 g) small tomatoes, sliced

1 lb (500 g) zucchini (courgettes), sliced

2 tablespoons thyme

1/3 cup (1 1/2 oz/45 g) grated Parmesan cheese

Heat 3 tablespoons of oil in a frying pan and add the onions, garlic, and bell peppers. Cook over medium heat for 5 minutes, stirring frequently, until the vegetables are soft.

Preheat an oven to 350°F (180°C/Gas Mark 4).

Cover the bottom of an 8-cup (2 qt/2 l) baking dish with the sautéed vegetables, then arrange the tomatoes and zucchini on top in rows. Sprinkle with the thyme and drizzle with 3/4 cup (6 fl oz/190 ml) olive oil. Bake for 30 minutes. Remove the dish from the oven, sprinkle with Parmesan cheese, and drizzle

with 1 tablespoon of oil. Bake for 15 minutes and serve hot.

Serves 6 as an accompaniment

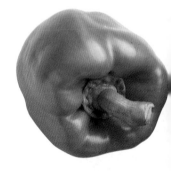

DESSERTS

Pavlova

6 egg whites

Pinch of cream of tartar

1 teaspoon vinegar

2 tablespoons low-calorie sweetener, suitable for cooking

1/4 teaspoon vanilla extract

1 cup whipped cream

6 passionfruit, to serve

1 prepared fruit-flavored, low-calorie (diet) gelatin dessert mix, chopped, to serve

Preheat an oven to 300°F (150°C/Gas Mark 2).

Beat the egg whites with the cream of tartar until stiff peaks form. Fold in the vanilla extract, vinegar, and sugar substitute and beat again until stiff. Spoon the mixture into a shaped springform pan, spreading the mixture so there is a slight well in the center.

Place the pavlova in the oven and immediately reduce the heat to 250°F (120°C/Gas Mark 1). Bake for about 1 1/2 hours. Remove from the oven and cool. Serve with the cream, gelatin dessert, and passionfruit on top.

Serves 4 to 6

Cheese Platter

A selection of blue and hard cheeses, such as Stilton or other blue cheese, goat cheese, Fontina, Cheddar, Gruyére, or Port-Salut (about 4 oz/125 g cheese per person)

Grape leaves, for garnish (optional)

Vegetable sticks, fresh fruit, and nuts to accompany

Present the cheeses simply on a tray, platter, or small marble or wooden cutting board, lining the surface with grape leaves.

Make it easy for guests to help themselves by including a sharp, broad-bladed knife for hard cheeses, a sharp knife with a pronged tip for semihard cheeses, and a blunt-bladed knife for soft cheeses.

Serve the cheeses with sticks of vegetables, such as celery, carrot, or radish. Or serve fresh fruits, such as grapes, apples, pears, and dates; or nuts, such as walnuts or pecans.

Serves 4 to 6

Mocha Cream Delight

1 tablespoon good-quality unsweetened cocoa powder, plus extra for decoration

2 tablespoons very strong coffee

Liquid sweetener equivalent to 6 teaspoons sugar, or to taste

½ teaspoon vanilla essence

1 cup (8 oz/250 g) heavy (double) cream, chilled

Dissolve the cocoa power in the coffee. Add the sweetener and vanilla. Refrigerate until cool.

Whip the cream. Add the cocoa and coffee mixture and whip again until stiff.

Spoon into glasses and chill well. Before serving, sift a little extra cocoa powder over the top.

Serves 4

Pears with Balsamic Vinegar and Goat Cheese

4 ripe pears, such as Bosc or Bartlett

1 tablespoon canola oil

1 tablespoon fresh lemon juice

4 oz (125 g) aged goat cheese, cut into 4 pieces

4 teaspoons good-quality balsamic vinegar

Trim the stems and bottoms off of the pears and peel. With a melon baller, scoop the cores from the bottoms of the pears. Cut each pear lengthwise into 8 slices about 3/4 inch (2 cm) thick. In a large bowl, combine the oil and lemon juice. Add the pear slices and toss them to coat.

Heat a nonstick frying pan over medium heat, add the pears and cook, in batches if necessary, until lightly browned, gently turning to brown evenly. Remove the pears from the pan and keep them warm. Repeat with the remaining pears.

Arrange the pears and the goat cheese on 4 dessert plates. Drizzle each serving with 1 teaspoon balsamic vinegar and serve.

Serves 4

Coconut Tofu

1 lb (500 g) silken tofu (bean curd)

Sweetener, to taste

Zest of 1 orange

2 tablespoons shredded coconut

2 tablespoons crushed hazelnuts

Process the tofu, sweetener, and orange zest for 10 minutes in a blender or food processor (this is important for texture and taste). Stir in the coconut.

Transfer to a decorative, glass serving dish and sprinkle with hazelnuts. Chill before serving.

Serves 4 to 6

Rhubarb Fool

4 cups (1 1/4 lb/600 g) rhubarb (ensure that all leaves and stem ends are trimmed off)

Sweetener, to taste

1 cup whipped cream, to serve

Place the rhubarb and sweetener in a saucepan, sprinkle with a little water, and bring to a boil. Cook for about 10 minutes, or until the rhubarb has softened. Cool.

Combine the rhubarb and cream and chill for at least 3 hours before serving.

Serves 2 to 4

Stewed Plums with Macadamia Nut Topping

1 vanilla bean

1/2 cup (4 fl oz/125 ml) water

1 teaspoon rosewater essence

4 plums, halved and pitted

1/3 cup (1 1/2 oz/45 g) macadamia nuts, finely crushed

2 tablespoons shredded coconut

Preheat an oven to 400°F (200°C/Gas Mark 5).

Place the vanilla bean, water, rosewater essence, and plums in a saucepan and simmer, covered, for about 10 minutes.

Meanwhile, mix together the nuts and coconut.

Place the plum halves on a lined baking tray, and fill the cavity of each half with the nut mixture.

Bake in the oven for 20 minutes, or until the nuts are toasted. Serve warm.

Serves 4

Baked Peach Crumble

4 peaches, halved and pitted

1 stick cinnamon

1¼ qt (1.25 l) low-calorie (diet) dry ginger ale

2 egg whites

⅓ cup (1½ oz/45 g) almond meal

Sweetener equivalent to 1 tablespoon sugar, or to taste

Heavy (double) cream or whipped cream, to serve

Preheat an oven to 300°F (150°C/Gas Mark 2).

Place the peaches in a saucepan with the cinnamon and dry ginger ale, bring to a boil, then lower the heat to a simmer and poach until just soft, about 10 minutes. Drain and place in a greased ovenproof dish.

Beat the egg whites until stiff. Fold almond meal and sweetener into the egg whites and spread on top of the peaches. Bake in the oven until the meringue has slightly browned.

Allow to cool, then serve with the cream.

Serves 4

Fruit Blancmange

1 envelope of fruit-flavored, low-calorie (diet) gelatin dessert mix

1 cup (8 oz/250 g) ricotta cheese

2 tablespoons cream

1 cup chopped fresh fruit, such as pineapple, peaches, or apricots

Make up the gelatin dessert mix as per the instructions, but with only two-thirds of the suggested liquid. Chill until almost set.

Beat the ricotta and cream together until smooth, and then beat into the gelatin dessert.

Stir the fruits through the mixture and then chill the dessert in the refrigerator until lightly set, before serving.

Serves 2 to 3

Pears with Mascarpone and Ginger

POACHED PEARS

2 large ripe pears

1 1/2 cups (12 fl oz/375 ml) Moscato d'Asti wine, or other sweet dessert wine

1 stick cinnamon, 3 inches (7.5 cm) long, broken in half

1/2 teaspoon allspice berries or 1 whole clove

MASCARPONE TOPPING

1/2 cup (3 oz/100 g) mascarpone cheese

1 tablespoon light (single) cream

Sweetener equivalent to 2 tablespoons sugar, or to taste

Candied ginger, chopped, for garnish (optional)

4 fresh mint sprigs, for garnish (optional)

To poach the pears, cut them in half lengthwise, then core and peel the halves. In a saucepan, combine the wine, cinnamon, and allspice berries or the clove, and bring to a boil. Place the pears in the liquid, cored side down, reduce the heat to medium-low, and simmer for 4–5 minutes. Turn the pears over and poach until barely soft when pierced with a sharp knife, 4–5 minutes longer.

Using a slotted spoon, carefully place each pear half, cored side down, in the center of an individual plate.

Reduce the poaching liquid over medium heat until it forms a thick syrup, about 5 minutes. Strain through a fine-mesh sieve into a clean container. Discard the contents of the sieve.

For the mascarpone topping, in a small bowl, whisk together the mascarpone, cream, and sweetener until smooth.

To serve, cut each pear half into a fan shape: Hold a paring knife at a 45-degree angle to the pear, and make slashes completely through it, but leave the top intact. Gently press on the slices of pear to fan them out, and then drizzle the reduced syrup over the top.

Place a dollop of the mascarpone mixture at the top of each pear. Sprinkle evenly with the candied ginger and garnish with the mint sprigs, if desired. Serve.

Serves 4

Fruit Kabobs

4 cups (1½ lb/750 g) cubed pineapple, cubed melon, halved strawberries, and mandarin segments

1 glass sherry, mixed with ½ teaspoon cinnamon

Whipped cream, to serve (optional)

Soak 8 wooden skewers in cold water for at least 20 minutes.

Marinate the fruit in the cinnamon-infused sherry for at least 1 hour.

Thread the cubes of fruit onto the skewers and place under a broiler (griller) or on a grill (barbecue). Cook, brushing with the remaining marinade and turning frequently to prevent burning, until lightly browned, 3–4 minutes.

Serve the skewers with whipped cream, if desired.

Serves 4

Raspberry Parfait

1 cup (8 oz/250 g) cottage cheese

Sweetener, to taste

1 cup (8 fl oz/250 ml) light (single) cream, whipped

2 egg whites, whipped with a pinch of salt until stiff

1 cup (4 oz/125 g) raspberries, mashed

Beat the cottage cheese and sweetener together until smooth. Fold in the whipped cream and then the egg whites. Gently mix through the raspberries.

Transfer to a glass serving bowl and chill for several hours in the refrigerator before serving.

Serves 4 to 6

Glossary

The following glossary provides advice on selecting, storing, and preparing some of the ingredients used in this book.

ARTICHOKES

Native to the Mediterranean, prickly artichokes look like tall thistles. The fleshy base of the inner leaves and the bottom of the bud are tender when cooked; the remainder, including the rest of the leaf and the fuzzy interior choke, are discarded. Fresh artichokes are sold all year in various sizes. Select compact, heavy globes with tightly closed leaves; store in a plastic bag, refrigerated, for up to 4 days.

artichokes

ARUGULA

Also known as rocket, this green leaf vegetable has slender, multiple-lobed leaves and a peppery, slightly bitter flavor. Use raw in salads, sandwiches, and other savory dishes.

ASPARAGUS

These tender stalks are prized for their delicate flavor and marvelous green hue, sometimes tinged with purple at the cap (white asparagus, a delicacy, is much less common). Crisp, straight, firm stalks with tight buds are best. Store wrapped in damp paper towels in a plastic bag, refrigerated, for up to 4 days.

BALSAMIC VINEGAR

This is a specialty of the Italian region of Emilia-Romagna, primarily in the town of Modena. It is an aged vinegar made from the pure wine must (unfermented grape juice) of white Trebbiano grapes. It is aged in wooden casks for as little as 1 year or for as much as 75 years or even longer, slowly evaporating and growing sweeter and mellower with time. Long-aged balsamic vinegar is an intense, expensive, syrupy vinegar that should be used sparingly. Younger balsamic vinegar makes a superb salad dressing and is used, often reduced, in sauces for other foods, or is sprinkled over fruit.

BELL PEPPERS (CAPSICUMS)

Bell peppers are actually fruits, although they are eaten as vegetables. Crunchy and colorful, they are related to chilies, but are far milder in taste. They change color as they ripen, from green to orange, yellow, red, or purple. They can be eaten raw, added to salads, or cooked, when they become much sweeter and softer. Store uncut fruits in a plastic bag in the refrigerator for up to 1 week.

CANOLA OIL

This is a bland oil pressed from rapeseed, a relative of the mustard plant. It is high in monounsaturated fat. It is good for general cooking and baking, but can smell unpleasant at high frying temperatures.

CAPERS

The buds of a Mediterranean bush. A savory flavoring, they are most commonly pickled in salt and vinegar. They add a pleasantly pungent flavor and a light crunch to meat, fish, and egg dishes, and to various sauces.

asparagus

CHIVES

The long, hollow green leaves of this herb add bright color and a mild onion flavor to many dishes. Fresh chives should not be wilted or damaged. Wrap in damp paper towels and store in a plastic bag in the refrigerator for up to 4 days. Chop chives finely and add them at the end of the cooking time so that their delicate flavor is not destroyed.

CILANTRO (FRESH CORIANDER)

This strongly flavored herb is very popular in Asian, Indian, Latin American, and Middle Eastern cooking. To store, rinse under cold running water, shake dry, then wrap in paper towels and refrigerate in a plastic bag for up to 1 week.

FINES HERBES

This is a traditional mixture of finely chopped herbs, usually parsley, chives, chervil, and tarragon. However, marjoram, savory, watercress, and burnet are sometimes used in the mix. Add fines herbes to the dish shortly before serving, as they lose their flavor if added too early during cooking. Fines herbes are left in the dish, not removed before serving like other herb mixes, such as bouquet garni.

mortar and pestle

GALANGAL

This rhizome is used widely in Asian cooking in a similar way to ginger, which it resembles in appearance and flavor. Fresh galangal can be difficult to find outside of Asia, but dried galangal is often stocked in Asian markets. Fresh ginger can be substituted if galangal is not available.

olive oil

Glossary

HOISIN SAUCE

This mixture of soybeans, garlic, chilies, and spices is usually used as a condiment. Bottled hoisin sauce will keep indefinitely if refrigerated once opened.

LEMONGRASS

An aromatic herb used throughout Southeast Asia, lemongrass flavors soups, curries, and grilled dishes. Resembling a green (spring) onion in shape, lemongrass has long, thin, gray-green leaves that meet and overlap along a woody stem. Look for firm stalks, with no sign of fading or drying.

MUSHROOMS

There are numerous varieties, colors, and sizes of edible fungi. Select firm, fresh, plump mushrooms that aren't bruised or slimy. Store in the refrigerator, lightly wrapped in paper towels or in a paper bag. Never store them in plastic, or they will sweat and perish. Use within 2 days.

OLIVE OIL

A staple of Mediterranean cooking, olive oil imparts a clean, fruity flavor and golden-to-green color to salad dressings, broiled (grilled) or grilled (barbecued) bread, and pasta sauces. Use extra virgin olive oils, from the first pressing, for cold dishes and for drizzling over food just before serving. For sauces and pan-frying, use olive oil labeled "pure" or "light." Store in a dark place away from heat for 6 months, or in the refrigerator for 1 year. (Chilled oil may become thick and cloudy; let it warm to room temperature before using.)

PANCETTA

This unsmoked Italian bacon is cured simply with salt and pepper. Fried with onions and other vegetables, it forms the basis for many Italian dishes.

PARSLEY

Widely used for cooking and as a garnish, parsley has such a clean, refreshing flavor that it is sometimes enjoyed as an after-meal digestive. Curly-leaf parsley is mild, while flat-leaf (Italian) parsley is more pungent. Select healthy, lively looking bunches. To store, rinse under cold running water and shake dry, then wrap in paper towels and keep in a plastic bag in the refrigerator for up to 1 week.

PROSCIUTTO

A specialty of Parma, a city in northern Italy, this raw ham is cured by dry-salting for 1 month, then air-drying in cool curing sheds for at least 6 months. It has a deep pink color and an intense flavor.

RICE WINE

A wine fermented from rice, this is usually low in alcohol. The most famous wines are probably the Japanese sake and mirin. There are many varieties of Chinese rice wine available in Asian markets.

SESAME SEEDS AND OIL

Sesame seeds are used in savory and sweet dishes alike. Sesame oil tastes of the seed from which it is produced and is used mainly as a seasoning for its nutty flavor.

SHALLOTS

These small cousins of the onion have a papery brown skin, purple-tinged flesh, and a flavor resembling both sweet onion and garlic.

TAMARIND

Also known as the Indian date, this is the fruit of a tree grown in Africa, Asia, and India. It produces pods (similar to a broad bean) that are sun-dried and then mixed with salt to form a smooth, dark brown, soft block. It can also be refined further to form a thick sauce, known as tamarind concentrate. Tamarind's unique, sweet-tart, fruity flavor is often used to give a sharp, tangy edge to curries and sauces.

TOFU

Tofu, or bean curd, is one of the many products made from the soybean. It comes in silken, soft, medium, firm, and extra-firm ivory-colored blocks and has a mild flavor. It comes packed in water and should be drained, rinsed, and then drained again before use.

TOMATOES

tomatoes

Although they are botanically a fruit, tomatoes are eaten as a vegetable. Oval-shaped plum (Roma) tomatoes are thick and meaty, with less juice and smaller seeds than other varieties, making them ideal for soups and stews. Store fresh tomatoes at room temperature for several days; do not refrigerate them, or their flavor and texture will suffer. Underripe tomatoes will ripen in a few days if left on a sunny windowsill or countertop. For most soups and stews, canned tomatoes are just as good as fresh ones.

Index

Entries in *italics* indicate illustrations and photos.

A

Almonds 271
Antipasto 126, 127
Artichokes, lamb stew with 172–3
Asparagus
　Dijon-herb mayonnaise, with 66, 67
　goat cheese, pancetta, and asparagus salad with vinaigrette 120, 121
　olive oil and parmesan, with 264, 265
　orange-sesame dressing, with 242–3, 243
　salad, warm mixed mushroom and 282, 283
　stir-fried with chicken 210, 211
Avocado
　chicken and mango salad with curry macadamia dressing 108–9, 109
　guacamole 73, 226–7

B

Bacon
　breakfast BLT 23

cheese and egg scramble with chives and 30, 31
　sautéed mushrooms and 33
Beans
　eggs scrambled with salsa and 28–9
　garlic green 248, 249
Beef
　coriander-crusted tenderloin with grilled green onions 152–3
　ginger stir-fry 170, 171
　grilled lemongrass 204–5, 205
　kabobs with minted coconut chutney 224–5, 225
　margarita steak with grilled onion guacamole 226–7
　mustard steaks 164
　Neapolitan braised beef braciole 208–9, 209
　rare roast, salad 106, 107
　rolls with blue cheese sauce 166, 167
　Thai beef salad 116–17
Bell peppers
　baby squash and yellow pepper salad with raspberry vinaigrette 284, 285

baked, and salami salad 122, 123
　caponata 262, 263
　coulis, stuffed chicken breasts with 10, 184–5, 185
　fish fillets with bell pepper coriander and lemon sauce 194, 195
　grilled vegetable salad 274–6, 275
　pork ragout with red 218–19, 219
　seafood gazpacho 68, 69
　summer ratatouille 277
　tomato and, soup with chili cream 64–5, 65
　vegetable omelet 88
　warm chicken and, salad 132, 133
Broccoli, Italian, with olives 267

C

Cabbage
　Chinese, with sesame seeds 266
　drunken pork with pears and 156–9, 157
　pork with crunchy red 147
　tricolor coleslaw 254, 255
Calcium, dietary 16

Carbohydrates 8–9, 14–15
Casserole, slow-cooked vegetable 256, 257
Cauliflower with garlic and paprika 288
Cheese
  beef rolls with blue cheese sauce 166, 167
  egg scramble with chives and bacon 30, 31
  goat cheese, pancetta, and asparagus salad with vinaigrette 120, 121
  grilled eggplant and goat cheese rolls 80–1, 81
  haloumi and vegetable kabobs 9, 82, 83
  pear, walnut, and blue cheese salad 272, 273
  pears with balsamic vinegar and goat cheese 298, 299
  pears with mascarpone and ginger 304–5
  platter 295
  prosciutto, pear, and parmesan salad 278, 279
  ricotta cheese scramble 40, 41
  smoked ham and camembert salad 110, 111
  tomato, mozzarella, and basil salad 252, 253
    tomato, prosciutto, and mozzarella salad with balsamic vinaigrette 268, 269
Chicken
  almond and, salad 118, 119
  antipasto 126, 127
  avocado and mango salad with curry macadamia dressing 108–9, 109
  blackened 230, 231
  bon-bon salad 102, 103
  butterflied citrus 142, 143
  cacciatore 182, 183
  curry with three accompaniments 178–80, 179
  firecracker chicken thighs 160, 161
  ginger, with mushrooms 187
  Greek-style salad 100–1, 101
  grilled five-spice 206, 207
  grilled sesame 146
  hearty casserole 222, 223
  Italian, with pesto mayonnaise 190–1, 191
  kaffir lime leaf, with 228–9, 229
  Mexican marinated 188, 189
  paprika (microwave) 199
  Provençal 200, 201
  rouladen 168–9, 169
  salad Niçoise 112–13, 113
    spiced lime salad 124–5, 125
  spicy Spanish kabobs 46, 47
  spicy yogurt 198
  stir-fried with asparagus 210, 211
  straw mushrooms, with 236, 237
  stuffed breasts with bell pepper coulis 10, 184–5, 185
  warm bell pepper and, salad 132, 133
  warm Thai salad 128–9, 128–9
  wings with barbecue sauce 17, 44, 45
Chili cream 64–5, 65
Chocolate
  mocha cream delight 296, 297
Cilantro see also Coriander
  mussels with tomato and 90, 91
  pesto with lime and chilies 75
Coconut tofu 300
Coriander see also Cilantro
  crusted beef tenderloin with grilled green onions 152–3
  fish fillets with bell pepper, coriander and lemon sauce 194, 195
Cucumber, relish 48–9
Curry
  chicken with three accompaniments 178–80, 179
  macadamia dressing 108–9, 109

D, E

Dips
cilantro pesto with lime and chilies 75
crab 72
guacamole 73
horseradish cream sauce 75
lemon vinaigrette 75
tapenade 73
Drinks
strawberry cream smoothie 36, 37
watermelon frappé 32, 32
Eggplant 89
baby eggplant salad 130, 131
caponata 262, 263
grilled rolls with goat cheese 80-1, 81
grilled vegetable salad 274-6, 275
Sicilian vegetable soup 54, 55
spicy sauce, in 246, 247
summer ratatouille 277
vegetable omelet 88
Eggs
Benedict with Virginia ham 38-9
cheese scramble with chives and bacon 30, 31
classic omelets with fines herbes and tomato concasse 20-2, 21
curried 26

florentine 24, 25
mushroom flan 92, 93
scrambled with beans and salsa 28-9

F

Fats, dietary 12-13
Fiber, importance of 34
Figs and prosciutto 94, 95
Fish see also Seafood
fish cakes with pickled cucumber relish 48-9
fillets with bell pepper, coriander and lemon sauce 194, 195
grilled in grape leaves 216, 217
grilled swordfish kabobs 148, 149
grilled tuna kabobs 181
lemon sole with salsa verde 165
sea perch with herb butter 186
sesame salmon steaks 144, 145
smoked salmon stack 27
soup 56-7, 57
sour fish soup 52-3
spicy grilled snapper with dill 233
swordfish with spinach and citrus vinaigrette 212-13, 213
trout wrapped in ham 174, 175
tuna salad 104-5, 105
Fruit
blancmange 303
kabobs 306

G

Garlic
cauliflower with paprika and 288
green beans 248, 249
lamb shoulder with thyme and 140-1, 141
shrimp with garlic and baked tomato 76-7, 77
Ginger 220
beef stir-fry 170, 171
chicken, with mushrooms 187
pears with mascarpone and 304-5
Greek salad 250, 251
Guacamole 73, 226-7

H

Haloumi and vegetable kabobs 9, 82, 83
Ham
chef's salad 114, 115
eggs Benedict with Virginia ham 38-9
goat cheese, pancetta, and asparagus salad with vinaigrette 120, 121
prosciutto and figs 94, 95
prosciutto-wrapped shrimp skewers 214-15
smoked, and camembert salad 110, 111

Ham *continued*
    trout wrapped in 174, *175*
Herbs *see also by name*
    classic omelets with fines herbes
        and tomato concasse 20–2, *21*
    grilled five-spice chicken *206, 207*
    grilled lemongrass beef 204–5,
        205
    herb butter 186
    onion and herb frittata 84, *85*
    spicy grilled snapper with dill 233
    tomato, mozzarella and basil salad
        252, *253*
Honey sauce, lamb in *154, 155*
Horseradish cream sauce 75

I, K
Italian
    chicken with pesto mayonnaise
        190–1, *191*
    sausage casserole 232
Kabobs
    beef with minted coconut chutney
        224–5, *225*
    grilled swordfish *148, 149*
    grilled tuna 181
    haloumi and vegetable *9, 82, 83*
    mixed meat *176, 177*
    spicy Spanish chicken *46, 47*
Kaffir lime leaf, chicken with 228–9,
    229

L
Lamb
    grilled stuffed leg of 162–3, *163*
    honey sauce, in *154, 155*
    Middle Eastern skewers 192–3
    roast lamb leg with yogurt 202–3
    shoulder with garlic and thyme
        140–1, *141*
    spicy soup 60–1
    stew with artichokes 172–3
Lemon
    fish fillets with bell pepper,
        coriander and lemon sauce *194*,
        195
    swordfish with spinach and citrus
        vinaigrette 212–13, *213*
    vinaigrette 75
Lime, spiced chicken and, salad
    124–5, *125*

M, N
Mango
    chicken and avocado salad with
        curry macadamia dressing
        108–9, *109*
    salsa, shrimp skewers with 196–7,
        197
Mayonnaise
    Dijon-herb *66, 67*
    pesto 190–1, *191*

Meat kabobs, mixed *176, 177*
Meatballs, spiced *70, 71*
Mediterranean scallop stew 150–1,
    151
Mexican marinated chicken *188, 189*
Middle Eastern lamb skewers 192–3
Minted coconut chutney 224–5, *225*
Mushrooms
    chicken with straw *236, 237*
    egg and, flan 92, *93*
    ginger chicken with 187
    salad, warm mixed asparagus and
        282, *283*
    sautéed with bacon 33
    sautéed with garlic *244*, 245
    stuffed field *86*, 87
    wild mushroom soup 96, *97*
Mustard steaks 164
Neapolitan braised beef braciole
    208–9, *209*

O, P
Okra with tomatoes 289
Orange-sesame dressing, asparagus
    with 242–3, *243*
Paprika
    cauliflower with garlic and 288
    chicken (microwave) 199
Parmesan, asparagus with olive oil
    and *264*, 265
Pavlova 294

Peach crumble, baked 302
Pears
    balsamic vinegar and goat cheese,
        with 298, 299
    cabbage with drunken pork and
        156–9, 157
    mascarpone and ginger, with
        304–5
    salad, prosciutto, parmesan, and
        278, 279
    walnut and blue cheese salad 272,
        273
Pesto mayonnaise, Italian chicken
    with 190–1, 191
Plums, stewed, with macadamia nut
    topping 301
Pork
    crunchy red cabbage, with 147
    drunken pork with cabbage and
        pears 156–9, 157
    ragout with red bell peppers
        218–19, 219
Prosciutto
    figs and 94, 95
    salad, pear, parmesan and 278, 279
    tomato and mozzarella salad with
        balsamic vinaigrette 268, 269
    wrapped shrimp skewers 214–15
Protein, dietary 10–11
Provençal chicken 200, 201
Pumpkin soup 78, 79

R
Ragout, pork with red bell peppers
    218–19, 219
Raspberry
    parfait 307
    vinaigrette 284, 285
Ratatouille, summer 277
Rhubarb fool 300
Rosemary
    roast leg of lamb with yogurt
        202–3

S
Saffron mussel stew 234–5, 235
Salads see also Vegetables
    antipasto 126, 127
    baby eggplant 130, 131
    baby squash and yellow pepper
        with raspberry vinaigrette 284,
        285
    baked red bell pepper and salami
        122, 123
    bon-bon chicken 102, 103
    chef's 114, 115
    chicken and almond 118, 119
    chicken, avocado and mango
        with curry macadamia dressing
        108–9, 109
    chicken Niçoise 112–13, 113

goat cheese, pancetta, and
    asparagus with vinaigrette 120,
    121
Greek 250, 251
Greek-style chicken 100–1, 101
grilled vegetable 274–6, 275
pear, walnut and blue cheese 272,
    273
prosciutto, pear and parmesan
    278, 279
rare roast beef 106, 107
roasted tomato 286, 287
smoked ham and camembert 110,
    111
spiced lime chicken 124–5, 125
spring vegetable 134, 135
stuffed tomato 136, 137
summer vegetable 280, 281
Thai beef 116–17
tomato, mozzarella and basil 252,
    253
tricolor coleslaw 254, 255
tuna 104–5, 105
warm chicken and bell pepper
    132, 133
warm mixed mushroom and
    asparagus 282, 283
warm Thai chicken 128–9, 128–9
Salami and baked red bell pepper
    salad 122, 123
Salsa verde 165

Sausage
  Italian casserole 232
  stewed clams, tomatoes and
    238–9, *239*
Seafood *see also* Fish
  clear broth with grilled seafood
    62, *63*
  crab dip 72
  crab patties 35
  shrimp with fresh herbs 58, *59*
  gazpacho 68, *69*
  Mediterranean scallop stew
    150–1, *151*
  mussels with cilantro and tomato
    90, *91*
  oysters with dipping sauces 74, *75*
  prosciutto-wrapped shrimp
    skewers 214–15
  saffron mussel stew 234–5, *235*
  shrimp skewers with mango salsa
    196–7, *197*
  shrimp with garlic and baked
    tomato 76–7, *77*
  stewed clams, sausage and
    tomatoes 238–9, *239*
  stir-fried shrimp with vegetables
    221
Sesame
  Chinese cabbage with sesame
    seeds 266
  grilled chicken 146

orange-sesame dressing, asparagus
  with 242–3, *243*
salmon steaks 144, *145*
Soups
  broth with grilled seafood 62, *63*
  fish 56–7, *57*
  fresh tomato and thyme 50, *51*
  pumpkin 78, *79*
  seafood gazpacho 68, *69*
  Sicilian vegetable 54, *55*
  sour fish 52–3
  spicy lamb 60–1
  tomato and bell pepper, with chili
    cream 64–5, *65*
  wild mushroom 96, *97*
Spiced meatballs 70, *71*
Spicy sauce, eggplant in 246, *247*
Spicy yogurt chicken 198
Spinach and citrus vinaigrette
  212–13, *213*
Squash
  baby squash and yellow pepper
    salad with raspberry vinaigrette
    284, 285
  summer vegetable salad *280*, 281
Stir-fry
  beef and ginger *170*, 171
  chicken and asparagus *210*, 211
  green vegetables 270
  shrimp with vegetables 221
Strawberry cream smoothie 36, *37*

T
Tapenade 73
Taste 17
Terrine, vegetable, with tomato sauce
  258–61, *259*
Thai salads 116–17, 128–9, *128–9*
Thyme
  fresh tomato soup 50, *51*
  lamb shoulder with garlic and
    thyme 140–1, *141*
Tomato
  bell pepper and, soup, with chili
    cream 64–5, *65*
  breakfast BLT 23
  caponata 262, *263*
  concasse 20–2, *21*
  fresh tomato and thyme soup 50,
    51
  gratin, zucchini and 290, *291*
  mozzarella and basil salad 252,
    253
  mussels with cilantro and 90, *91*
  okra with 289
  prosciutto and mozzarella salad
    with balsamic vinaigrette 268,
    269
  ricotta cheese scramble *40*, 41
  roasted tomato salad 286, *287*
  salsa 28–9
  seafood gazpacho 68, *69*

Tomato *continued*
 shrimp with garlic and baked 76–7, 77
 stewed clams, sausage and 238–9, 239
 stuffed tomato salad 136, *137*
 vegetable omelet 88
 vegetable terrine with tomato sauce 258–61, *259*

V

Vegetables *see also by name*
 caponata 262, *263*
 cauliflower with garlic and paprika 288
 fish cakes with pickled cucumber relish 48–9
 garlic green beans 248, *249*
 grilled vegetable salad 274–6, *275*
 haloumi and vegetable kabobs 9, 82, *83*
 Italian broccoli with olives 267
 okra with tomatoes 289
 omelet 88
 onion and herb frittata 84, *85*
 pumpkin soup 78, *79*
 salads *see* Salads
 Sicilian vegetable soup *54*, 55
 slow-cooked vegetable casserole *256*, 257
 stir-fried green vegetables 270
 stir-fried shrimp with 221
 summer ratatouille 277
 swordfish with spinach and citrus vinaigrette 212–13, *213*
 terrine with tomato sauce 258–61, *259*
 tomato and bell pepper soup with chili cream 64–5, *65*
 tricolor coleslaw 254, *255*

W, Y, Z

Walnut, pear, and blue cheese salad 272, *273*
Watermelon frappé 32, *32*
Yogurt
 roast leg of lamb with 202–3
 spicy chicken 198
Zucchini
 gratin, tomato and 290, *291*
 grilled vegetable salad 274–6, *275*
 vegetable omelet 88

Acknowledgments

Weldon Owen would like to thank Tessy Grabo and Grace Newell, for editorial assistance, and Puddingburn Publishing Services, for compiling the index.

Photography Ad-Libitum/Stuart Bowey, John Callanan, Kevin Candland, Rowan Fotheringham, John Hollingshead, Peter Johnson, Valerie Martin, Joyce Oudkerk Pool, Penina, Alejandro Pradera, Chris Shorten.

Styling Janice Baker, Penny Farrell, Kay Francis, Stephanie Greenleigh, Jane Hann, Susan Massey, Sally Parker, Pouké, Vicki Roberts-Russell.